NEW HAMLYN
ALL COLOUR
COOKBOOK

NEW HAMLYN
ALL COLOUR
COOKBOOK

Bounty Books

First published in Great Britain in 2003 by
Hamlyn, a division of Octopus Publishing Group Ltd

Reprinted in 2005, 2006, 2007 by Bounty Books

This edition published in 2010 by Bounty Books,
a division of Octopus Publishing Group Ltd
189 Shaftesbury Avenue
Endeavour House
London WC2H 8JY
www.octopusbooks.co.uk

An Hachette UK Company
www.hachette.co.uk

Copyright © Octopus Publishing Group Ltd 2003

ISBN 978-0-753719-64-0

A CIP catalogue record for this book is available from
the British Library

Printed in China

Executive Editor **Nicola Hill**
Executive Art Editor **Geoff Fennell**
Editor **Katy Denny**
Designer **Nigel Soper**
Picture Librarian **Jennifer Veall**
Picture Library Assistant **Luzia Strohmayer**
Production Controller **Ian Paton**

Contents

Introduction

In the decades since the original edition of the *Hamlyn All Colour Cookbook* was published, cooking and eating habits have undergone a sea-change. Gone are the days when families sat down together to eat a meal prepared from a fairly limited range of ingredients bought from the local butcher and greengrocer. Over the past 30 years, people have begun to rely on ready-prepared, supermarket-made meals for one or two or on take-away foods, and local stores have all but disappeared. At the same time, increased awareness of food from other countries has seen curries, pizzas and stir-fries gain a regular place in our diets, and dishes that were at one time regarded with suspicion, such as those containing garlic, have become commonplace on dining tables. So why bother cooking at all when it is so easy to buy such a wide range of delicious, ready-prepared meals?

Recently, there has been a revival of interest in preparing and cooking food at home. Food scares and concerns about chemical additives and allergic reactions to a range of ingredients have coincided with advice from dieticians and nutritionists that we should eat a varied diet, including at least five portions of fresh fruit and vegetables every day. We are told that ready-prepared meals contain hidden quantities of salt, sugar, preservatives, colorants and other additives, and we know that mass-produced fruit and vegetables are treated to enhance their appearance and prolong their shelf-life. We are increasingly aware of the ways in which food is brought to our tables and, at the same time, increasingly concerned to know just what it is we are eating.

Supermarkets are still most people's main source of food. Most of them stock both staple foods – from vegetables, fish and meat to bread, milk and eggs – and more exotic ingredients such as lemon grass, venison and pak choi. However, interest in preparing and cooking meals from fresh ingredients, often bought locally or from a known source, has increased interest in the idea of seasonality – buying and eating produce when it is naturally available. As testament to this, farmers' markets are growing in number around the country, where the produce is often organic and always seasonal.

Recipes

The recipes included in this new edition of the *All Colour Cookbook* have been carefully selected to reflect the current resurgence of interest in food and cooking. From soups to cakes, the recipes use a wide range of fresh ingredients. International dishes are, of course, well represented. Indian, Italian and Oriental food now plays an important part in our diet – indeed, an entire section is devoted to pizza, noodles, pasta and rice. There is also a section for vegetarians, whose numbers continue to increase, as well as recipes for using vegetables, as both accompaniments for main dishes and in salads, in unusual and interesting ways. Meat and fish dishes are also well represented. There are old favourites, such as braised lamb, and also recipes for venison and duck, relative newcomers to the standard repertoire. The fish dishes range from new ways to use cod and haddock to those using the increasingly popular red snapper and squid.

Each recipe indicates the preparation and cooking time for the dish. These are intended for guidance only, and cooking times in particular will vary from appliance to appliance. All the ingredients are listed in the order they are used. Quantities are given in both metric and imperial versions, but keep to one system or the other.

Equipment

All the recipes in this book can be made with the equipment found in an average kitchen. Although a food processor or blender will shorten the preparation time of some of the recipes in this book, none of them require specialist equipment – soups can be pressed through sieves, and batters and cakes blended and beaten by hand. Similarly, if you like pasta you may have a special machine to make the fresh product, but there are so many good-quality dried pastas as well as fresh pasta from specialist stores or even the chiller cabinets of some supermarkets that you can try all the recipes here with confidence. Simply adapt the cooking time to suit the type of pasta you are using.

Ingredients

Always use the best quality ingredients you can afford and, whenever possible, buy the amount you need rather than large quantities that you have to store. Olive oil, once regarded as an exotic addition to southern European dishes, is now widely available in a range of qualities. If you are using oil as part of a dressing for a salad or drizzling it over a dish, use extra virgin oil – the flavour is worth the additional expense. However, when you are using oil to soften onions or to seal meat, use your favourite oil or fat.

Remember, cooking need not be a chore. It can easily be as much of a pleasure to prepare a meal as it is to eat it. Enjoy!

Stocks

Most of the recipes in this book are self-contained and can be made without reference to other sections of the book, but many of the soups, and some of the meat dishes, use stock. Although you can, of course, make up the required quantity of stock from cubes or powder, home-made stock will give a recipe extra depth of flavour – and you can be sure that there is no extra salt or colouring. Making your own stock is well worth the time and small amount of effort involved. If you do not already have your own favourite stock recipe, use one of the following as directed in the recipe.

Beef stock

Preparation time: **15 minutes**	**750 g (1½ lb) shin of beef, cubed**
	2 onions, chopped
	2–3 carrots, chopped
Cooking time: **about 4¼ hours**	**2 celery sticks, chopped**
	1 bay leaf
	1 bouquet garni
Makes: **about 1.5 litres (2½ pints)**	**4–6 black peppercorns**
	1.8 litres (3 pints) water
	½ teaspoon salt

Place all the ingredients in a large saucepan. Bring to the boil slowly and immediately reduce the heat to a slow simmer. Cover the pan with a well-fitting lid and simmer for 4 hours, removing any scum that rises to the surface. Strain the stock through a muslin-lined sieve and leave to cool before refrigerating.

Chicken stock

Preparation time: **5–10 minutes**	**1 cooked chicken carcass**
	raw giblets and trimmings (optional)
	1 onion, chopped
Cooking time: **about 2½ hours**	**2–3 carrots, chopped**
	1 celery stick, chopped
	1 bay leaf
Makes: **about 1 litre (1¾ pints)**	**3–4 parsley stalks**
	1 thyme sprig
	1.8 litres (3 pints) water

Chop the chicken carcass into three or four pieces and place them in a large saucepan with the rest of the ingredients. Bring to the boil, removing any scum that rises to the surface. Lower the heat and simmer for 2–2½ hours. Strain the stock through a muslin-lined sieve and leave to cool before refrigerating.

Fish stock

Preparation time: **10 minutes**	**1.5 kg (3 lb) fish trimmings, from any fish apart from oily fish**
	1 onion, sliced
Cooking time: **about 30 minutes**	**1 small leek, white part only, sliced**
	1 celery stick, chopped
	1 bay leaf
Makes: **about 1.8 litres (3 pints)**	**6 parsley stalks**
	10 whole peppercorns
	475 ml (16 fl oz) dry white wine
	1.8 litres (3 pints) water

Place all the ingredients in a large saucepan. Bring slowly to just below boiling point and simmer very gently for 20 minutes, removing any scum that rises to the surface. Strain the stock through a muslin-lined sieve and leave to cool before refrigerating.

Vegetable stock

Preparation time: **5–10 minutes**	**500 g (1 lb) mixed vegetables (excluding potatoes, parsnips and other starchy root vegetables), chopped**
Cooking time: **about 40 minutes**	**1 garlic clove**
	6 peppercorns
	1 bouquet garni
Makes: **1 litre (1¾ pints)**	**1.2 litres (2 pints) water**

Place all the ingredients in a large saucepan. Bring to the boil and simmer gently for 30 minutes, skimming if necessary. Strain the stock through a muslin-lined sieve and leave to cool before refrigerating.

1 Soups

1 Fresh tomato soup   2 Gazpacho

1 Fresh tomato soup

Preparation time:
20 minutes

Cooking time:
35 minutes

Serves: 8

1 kg (2 lb) ripe tomatoes, coarsely chopped
1 small onion, chopped
1 tablespoon vegetable oil
1 sugar cube
1 orange
1.8 litres (3 pints) Chicken Stock or Vegetable Stock (see introduction)
2 cloves
1 bouquet garni
fresh thyme leaves, to garnish

Soften the tomatoes and onion in the oil for about 8 minutes. Rub the sugar cube over the orange peel to absorb the zest and add with the remaining ingredients to the tomato mixture. Bring to the boil, cover the pan and simmer gently for 25 minutes. Remove and discard the cloves and bouquet garni.

Purée the soup in a blender or food processor or push through a fine sieve. Reheat and serve, garnished with thyme leaves.

COOK'S NOTES A bouquet garni usually consists of a bay leaf, a sprig of thyme and 3 parsley stalks. It is often enclosed in a piece of celery or leek and tied with string, or it can be wrapped in a small square of muslin, tied with thin string.

2 Gazpacho

Preparation time:
15 minutes,
plus chilling

Serves: 6

1 garlic clove, chopped
¼ teaspoon salt
3 thick slices of white bread, crusts removed
1 kg (2 lb) ripe tomatoes, skinned and coarsely chopped
2 onions, coarsely chopped
½ large cucumber, peeled, deseeded and coarsely chopped
3 large green peppers, peeled, deseeded and coarsely chopped
5 tablespoons olive oil
4 tablespoons white wine vinegar
1 litre (1¾ pints) water
black pepper

Combine the chopped garlic and salt in a mortar and pound with a pestle until it is smooth. Alternatively, place the garlic and salt on a board and crush the garlic with the flattened blade of a knife.

Place the bread in a bowl and cover with cold water. Soak for 5 seconds, then drain the bread, squeezing out the moisture.

Set aside a quarter of the tomatoes, onions, cucumber and peppers for the garnish. Place the remaining vegetables in a blender or food processor and add the garlic paste, bread and oil. Purée the mixture until it is smooth.

Pour the mixture into a bowl and stir in the vinegar and water. Add pepper to taste. Cover closely with clingfilm and chill in the refrigerator for at least 3 hours.

Finely chop the reserved vegetables and serve them separately in small bowls with the soup.

Serve the soup very cold in individual bowls. Each guest adds a selection of the vegetable accompaniments to his or her portion.

3 French onion soup

4 Courgette and dill soup

Preparation time:	**50 g (2 oz) butter**
15 minutes	**750 g (1½ lb) onions, finely sliced**
	2 teaspoons sugar
Cooking time:	**2 teaspoons plain flour**
1 hour	**1 litre (1¾ pints) Chicken Stock or Beef**
	Stock (see introduction)
Serves: **4–5**	**½ small baguette, sliced**
	50 g (2 oz) Gruyère, grated
	salt and pepper
	chopped parsley, to garnish

Melt the butter in a saucepan and add the onions and sugar. Lower the heat to a bare simmer and cook the onions slowly for 20–30 minutes until they are soft and a really deep golden-brown. Stir occasionally and take care that they cook to a good colour without burning.

Stir the flour into the onion mixture and cook over a very low heat for about 5 minutes, stirring well to prevent it burning or sticking to the bottom of the pan.

Add the stock and season to taste. Increase the heat and bring to the boil, stirring, then reduce the heat and simmer for 15–20 minutes. Taste the soup and add more salt and pepper if necessary.

Meanwhile, toast the slices of baguette lightly on both sides. Place a piece of toast in each soup bowl and sprinkle the grated Gruyère on top. Ladle the hot soup over the bread and garnish with the parsley.

Preparation time:	**2–3 tablespoons sunflower oil or light**
20 minutes	**olive oil**
	1 large onion, chopped
Cooking time:	**2 garlic cloves, crushed**
30–40 minutes	**1 kg (2 lb) courgettes, sliced**
	1.2–1.5 litres (2–2½ pints) Vegetable
Serves: **8**	**Stock or Chicken Stock (see**
	introduction)
	2–4 tablespoons finely chopped dill
	salt and pepper

TO GARNISH:
125 ml (4 fl oz) single cream
dill fronds

Heat the oil in a saucepan and fry the onion and garlic until soft but not browned. Add the courgettes, cover the pan with greaseproof paper and cook over a low heat for 10–15 minutes until the courgettes are soft. Add the stock, cover the pan with a lid and simmer for a further 10–15 minutes.

Using a slotted spoon, transfer the courgettes and a little of the liquid to a blender or food processor. Purée until smooth, then pour into a clean saucepan. Add the remaining liquid and the chopped dill. Season to taste and bring to the boil.

Serve the soup in individual bowls, garnished with a swirl of cream and some dill fronds.

COOK'S NOTES The bread does not have to be perfectly fresh, so this is a good way to use up day-old bread which is past its best.

5 Cream of sweetcorn soup

6 Mushroom hot and sour soup

Preparation time:
5–10 minutes

Cooking time:
about 30 minutes

Serves: **4–6**

40 g (1½ oz) butter
1 onion, chopped
2 potatoes, diced
25 g (1 oz) plain flour
900 ml (1½ pints) milk
1 bay leaf
2 x 325 g (11 oz) cans sweetcorn, drained
2 tablespoons double cream
salt and pepper
fried bacon, crumbled, to garnish

Preparation time:
5 minutes

Cooking time:
20 minutes

Serves: **4**

1.2 litres (2 pints) Fish Stock (see introduction)
1 lemon grass stalk, lightly crushed
3 kaffir lime leaves or 3 pieces of lime peel
2 Thai red chillies, halved and deseeded
2 tablespoons lime juice
2 tablespoons Thai fish sauce
50 g (2 oz) canned bamboo shoots
125 g (4 oz) oyster mushrooms
2 spring onions, finely sliced
½ red chilli, sliced, to garnish

Melt the butter in a large saucepan. Add the onion and cook over a low heat, stirring frequently, for 5 minutes, without browning. Add the potatoes and cook for a further 2 minutes.

Stir in the flour, then gradually add the milk, stirring constantly. Bring to the boil, add the bay leaf and season to taste. Add half of the sweetcorn, cover the pan and simmer for 15–20 minutes.

Remove and discard the bay leaf and set the soup aside to cool slightly. Purée the soup in a blender or food processor or rub it through a sieve until smooth. Return it to the pan, add the remaining sweetcorn and heat through.

Stir in the cream, sprinkle over the bacon and serve immediately.

Pour the fish stock into a saucepan, add the lemon grass, lime leaves or peel and chillies. Simmer for 10 minutes. Strain the liquid into a clean saucepan. Reserve a little of the red chilli and discard the remaining seasonings.

Add the lime juice and fish sauce to the stock with the bamboo shoots, mushrooms and reserved chilli. Simmer for 5 minutes. Spoon into individual bowls and sprinkle with the spring onions. Garnish with fresh red chilli slices and serve.

7 Red pepper and ginger soup

8 Pumpkin and lemon soup

Preparation time: **20 minutes, plus cooling**	**3 red peppers, halved, cored and deseeded**
	1 red onion, quartered
	2 garlic cloves
Cooking time: **45 minutes**	**1 teaspoon olive oil**
	5 cm (2 inches) fresh root ginger, grated
	1 teaspoon ground cumin
Oven temperature: **200°C (400°F) Gas Mark 6**	**1 teaspoon ground coriander**
	1 large potato, chopped
	900 ml (1½ pints) Vegetable Stock (see introduction)
Serves: **4**	**4 tablespoons fromage frais**
	salt and pepper

Place the peppers, onion and garlic cloves in a nonstick roasting tin. Roast in a preheated oven, 200°C (400°F), Gas Mark 6, for 40 minutes or until the peppers have blistered and the onion quarters and garlic are soft. If the onion quarters start to brown too much, cover them with the pepper halves and continue cooking.

Meanwhile, heat the oil in a saucepan and fry the ginger, cumin and coriander over a low heat for 5 minutes, until softened. Add the potato, stir well and season to taste. Add the stock, cover the pan and simmer for 30 minutes.

Remove the cooked vegetables from the oven. Place the peppers in a polythene bag, tie the top and leave to cool. (The steam produced in the bag makes it easier to remove the skin when cool.) Add the onions to the potato mixture and carefully squeeze out the garlic pulp into the saucepan. Remove the skins from the peppers and add all but one half to the soup. Simmer for 5 minutes.

Purée the soup in a food processor or blender until quite smooth. Alternatively, rub through a fine sieve. Return to the saucepan and thin with a little water, if necessary, to achieve the desired consistency.

Spoon into individual bowls. Slice the remaining pepper and place the strips on top of the soup with a spoonful of fromage frais.

Preparation time: **30 minutes**	**50 g (2 oz) butter**
	1 large onion, sliced
	500 g (1 lb) pumpkin, peeled, deseeded and cut into chunks
Cooking time: **40 minutes**	**250 g (8 oz) potatoes, sliced**
	1 small garlic clove, crushed
Serves: **6**	**1 thyme sprig, plus extra to garnish**
	1.2 litres (2 pints) Chicken Stock (see introduction)
	juice of 1 lemon
	150 ml (¼ pint) double cream
	salt and pepper

Melt the butter in a large saucepan, add the onion and cook over a gentle heat until soft and transparent.

Add the pumpkin, potatoes, garlic and thyme, cover the pan and cook slowly for 20 minutes or until the vegetables are soft.

Add the stock and season to taste. Bring to the boil and simmer for 10 minutes. Remove the thyme sprig.

Purée the soup in a blender or food processor or rub through a sieve. Flavour the soup with lemon juice. Stir in the cream and reheat without boiling, then pour into individual bowls and serve garnished with a thyme sprig. Alternatively, reserve a little of the cream and swirl it over the soup in the bowls.

9 Butternut squash and rosemary soup

10 Celeriac and apple soup

Preparation time: **15 minutes**	**1 butternut squash** **a few rosemary sprigs, plus extra to garnish**
Cooking time: **1 hour 10 minutes**	**150 g (5 oz) red lentils, washed** **1 onion, finely chopped** **900 ml (1½ pints) Vegetable Stock (see introduction)**
Oven temperature: **200°C (400°F)** **Gas Mark 6**	**salt and pepper**

Serves: **4**

Halve the squash and use a spoon to scoop out the seeds and fibrous flesh. Peel and cut the squash into small chunks and place in a roasting tin. Sprinkle over the rosemary and season well. Roast in a preheated oven, 200°C (400°F), Gas Mark 6, for 45 minutes.

Meanwhile, place the lentils in a saucepan, cover with water, bring to the boil and boil rapidly for 10 minutes. Strain, then return the lentils to a clean saucepan with the onion and stock and simmer for 5 minutes. Season to taste.

Remove the squash from the oven, mash the flesh with a fork and add to the soup. Simmer for 25 minutes and then ladle into bowls. Garnish with more rosemary before serving.

Preparation time: **10–15 minutes**	**25 g (1 oz) butter or margarine** **1 celeriac, about 500 g (1 lb), peeled and chopped**
Cooking time: **about 35 minutes**	**3 dessert apples, peeled, cored and chopped**
Serves: **6**	**1.2 litres (2 pints) Chicken Stock or Vegetable Stock (see introduction)** **pinch of cayenne pepper, or more to taste** **salt and pepper**

TO GARNISH:
2–3 tablespoons finely diced dessert apple
paprika

Melt the butter or margarine in a large saucepan and cook the celeriac and apples over a moderate heat for 5 minutes or until they have begun to soften.

Add the stock and cayenne pepper and bring to the boil. Lower the heat, cover the pan and simmer for 25–30 minutes or until the celeriac and apples are very soft.

Purée the mixture in a blender or food processor until it is very smooth, transferring each batch to a clean saucepan. Alternatively, rub through a fine sieve. Reheat gently. Season to taste and serve in individual bowls, garnished with the finely diced apple and a dusting of paprika.

COOK'S NOTES Cayenne pepper is made from the dried and ground flesh and seeds of the bird's eye chilli. It is similar to chilli powder but not usually as hot. Paprika is made from mild varieties of sweet pepper, which have had their seeds removed before being dried and ground.

11 Roast root vegetable soup

12 Sweet potato soup

Preparation time: **10 minutes**	**4 carrots, chopped** **2 parsnips, chopped** **1 leek, finely chopped**
Cooking time: **1 hour 5 minutes**	**1.2 litres (2 pints) Vegetable Stock** **(see introduction)** **2 teaspoons thyme leaves**
Oven temperature: **200°C (400°F)** **Gas Mark 6**	**salt and pepper** **thyme sprigs, to garnish**
Serves: **6**	

Place the carrots and parsnips in a roasting tin and season with salt and pepper. Roast in a preheated oven, 200°C (400°F), Gas Mark 6, for 1 hour or until the vegetables are very soft.

Meanwhile, 20 minutes before the vegetables have finished roasting, put the leeks in a large saucepan with the stock and 1 teaspoon of the thyme. Cover the pan and simmer for 20 minutes.

Transfer the roasted root vegetables to a blender or food processor and blend, adding a little of the stock if necessary. Alternatively, rub through a fine sieve. Transfer to the stock saucepan and season to taste. Add the remaining thyme, stir and simmer for 5 minutes.

Ladle into individual bowls and serve garnished with the thyme sprigs.

COOK'S NOTES **Many different vegetables could be used in this soup. Try celeriac, pumpkin, fennel or courgettes as a variation.**

Preparation time: **20 minutes**	**25 g (1 oz) butter or margarine** **1 onion, chopped** **2 carrots, sliced**
Cooking time: **1 hour**	**2 celery sticks, sliced** **1 bay leaf**
Serves: **6–8**	**750 g (1½ lb) sweet potatoes, peeled** **and sliced**
	250 g (8 oz) potatoes, peeled and sliced **1.2 litres (2 pints) Chicken Stock (see** **introduction)** **150 ml (¼ pint) water** **125 ml (4 fl oz) dry white wine** **¼ teaspoon grated nutmeg** **¼ teaspoon white pepper** **4–6 rindless smoked bacon rashers,** **halved and grilled until crisp** **salt** **chopped parsley, to garnish**

Heat the butter or margarine in a frying pan and cook the onion, carrots, celery and bay leaf over a low heat for 5–8 minutes, stirring often.

Transfer the mixture to a saucepan. Add the sweet potatoes, potatoes, stock, water and white wine. Bring to the boil, then lower the heat and simmer, uncovered, for 35–40 minutes or until the vegetables are tender. Remove the bay leaf.

Purée the mixture, in batches if necessary, in a blender or food processor until smooth, transferring each batch to a clean saucepan. Alternatively, rub through a fine sieve. Add the nutmeg and pepper and season to taste with salt. Place the pan over a moderate heat and stir until the soup is hot.

Serve the soup in individual bowls topped with the bacon and garnished with parsley.

13 Chilli bean and pepper soup

14 Green lentil soup with spiced butter

Preparation time: **20 minutes**

Cooking time: **40 minutes**

Serves: **6**

2 tablespoons sunflower oil
1 large onion, finely chopped
4 garlic cloves, finely chopped
2 red peppers, cored, deseeded and diced
2 red chillies, deseeded and finely chopped
900 ml (1½ pints) Vegetable Stock (see introduction)
750 ml (1¼ pints) tomato juice or passata
1 tablespoon tomato purée
1 tablespoon sun-dried tomato paste
2 tablespoons sweet chilli sauce
400 g (13 oz) can red kidney beans, drained
2 tablespoons finely chopped fresh coriander
salt and pepper
75 ml (3 fl oz) soured cream

Preparation time: **10 minutes**

Cooking time: **25–30 minutes**

Serves: **4**

2 tablespoons extra virgin olive oil
2 onions, chopped
2 bay leaves
175 g (6 oz) green lentils, rinsed
1 litre (1¾ pints) Vegetable Stock (see introduction)
½ teaspoon ground turmeric
small handful of coriander leaves, roughly chopped
salt and pepper

SPICED BUTTER:
50 g (2 oz) lightly salted butter, softened
1 large garlic clove, crushed
2 tablespoons chopped fresh coriander
1 teaspoon paprika
1 teaspoon cumin seeds
1 red chilli, deseeded and finely chopped

Heat the oil in a large saucepan and fry the onion and garlic until soft but not coloured. Stir in the peppers and chillies and fry for a few minutes. Stir in the stock and tomato juice or passata, the tomato purée and paste, chilli sauce, kidney beans and coriander. Bring to the boil, cover the pan and simmer for 30 minutes.

Cool slightly, then purée in a blender or food processor until smooth. Alternatively, rub through a sieve. Return the soup to the pan and adjust the seasoning, adding a little extra chilli sauce if necessary. Bring to the boil and serve in individual bowls. Stir a little soured cream into each portion.

Heat the oil in a saucepan. Add the onions and cook for 3 minutes. Add the bay leaves, lentils, vegetable stock and turmeric. Bring to the boil, reduce the heat, cover the pan and simmer for 20 minutes or until the lentils are tender and turning mushy.

Meanwhile, make the spiced butter. Beat the butter with the garlic, coriander, paprika, cumin seeds and chilli and transfer to a small serving dish.

Stir the coriander leaves into the soup, season to taste and serve with the spiced butter in a separate bowl for stirring into the soup.

COOK'S NOTES Don't add salt to the soup until after the lentils have softened and are cooked through or their skins may remain tough.

15 Red lentil soup

16 Harira

Preparation time:
10 minutes

Cooking time:
25–30 minutes

Serves: 4

250 g (8 oz) split red lentils
1 leek, sliced
2 large carrots, sliced
1 celery stick, sliced
1 garlic clove, crushed (optional)
1 bay leaf
1.2 litres (2 pints) Vegetable Stock (see introduction)
½ teaspoon cayenne pepper
pepper

TO GARNISH:
natural yogurt
snipped chives or finely chopped parsley

Preparation time:
about 25 minutes,
plus soaking

Cooking time:
about 2¾ hours

Serves: 8–10

250 g (8 oz) chickpeas, soaked in cold water overnight
2 chicken breasts, halved
1.2 litres (2 pints) Chicken Stock (see introduction)
1.2 litres (2 pints) water
2 x 400 g (13 oz) cans chopped tomatoes
¼ teaspoon crumbled saffron threads (optional)
2 onions, chopped
125 g (4 oz) long-grain rice
50 g (2 oz) green lentils
2 tablespoons finely chopped coriander
2 tablespoons finely chopped parsley
salt and pepper
coriander sprigs, to garnish
natural yogurt, to serve

Place all the ingredients except the garnish in a large saucepan, bring to the boil, cover the pan and simmer for 20–25 minutes or until the lentils and vegetables are tender.

Allow the soup to cool slightly and remove the bay leaf. Purée the soup, in batches if necessary, in a blender or food processor until smooth. Alternatively, rub through a sieve.

Pour the soup into a clean saucepan, season with pepper and heat through. Serve in individual bowls, garnished with a spoonful of yogurt and a sprinkling of chives or parsley.

COOK'S NOTES Green lentils or yellow split peas could be used in this soup instead of the red lentils. You could also used dried beans, but soak them first overnight in a bowl of cold water and cook for longer, if necessary, to ensure they are soft.

Drain the chickpeas in a colander, rinse under cold running water and drain again. Place them in a saucepan, cover with 5 cm (2 inches) of water and bring to the boil. Lower the heat and simmer, partially covered, until tender, adding more water as necessary. This will take anything up to 2 hours. Drain the chickpeas and set aside.

Place the chicken breasts, stock and water in a second saucepan. Bring to the boil, lower the heat, cover the pan and simmer for 10–15 minutes or until the chicken is just cooked. Remove the chicken from the stock, place it on a board and shred it, discarding the skin. Set the shredded chicken aside.

Add the chickpeas, tomatoes, saffron (if using), onions, rice and lentils to the stock remaining in the pan. Cover the pan and simmer for 30–35 minutes or until the rice and lentils are tender.

Just before serving, add the shredded chicken, coriander and parsley. Heat the soup for a further 5 minutes without letting it boil. Season to taste and serve, garnished with coriander sprigs and drizzled with a little natural yogurt.

Preparation time:	**2 tablespoons olive oil**
5 minutes	**1 onion, chopped**
	1 garlic clove, crushed
Cooking time:	**2 celery sticks, chopped**
25 minutes	**1 leek, finely sliced**
	1 carrot, chopped
Serves: **4**	**400 g (13 oz) can chopped tomatoes**
	600 ml (1 pint) Chicken Stock or
	Vegetable Stock (see introduction)
	1 courgette, diced
	½ small cabbage, shredded
	1 bay leaf
	75 g (3 oz) canned haricot beans
	75 g (3 oz) dried spaghetti, broken into
	small pieces, or small pasta shapes
	1 tablespoon chopped flat leaf parsley
	salt and pepper
	50 g (2 oz) Parmesan, freshly grated,
	to serve

Heat the oil in a large saucepan. Add the onion, garlic, celery, leek and carrot and cook over a medium heat, stirring occasionally, for about 3 minutes.

Add the tomatoes, stock, courgette, cabbage, bay leaf and haricot beans. Bring to the boil, lower the heat and simmer for 10 minutes.

Add the pasta and season to taste. Stir well and cook for a further 8 minutes. Keep stirring because the soup may stick to the base of the pan. Just before serving, add the parsley and stir well. Ladle into individual bowls and serve with grated Parmesan.

Preparation time:	**2 tablespoons olive oil**
15 minutes	**1 large onion, chopped**
	2 garlic cloves, chopped
Cooking time:	**500 g (1 lb) potatoes, peeled and cut into**
40 minutes	**2.5 cm (1 inch) cubes**
	1.2 litres (2 pints) Vegetable Stock (see
Serves: **6**	**introduction) or water**
	250 g (8 oz) spring greens, finely
	shredded
	2 tablespoons chopped parsley
	salt and pepper
	croûtons, to serve

Heat the olive oil in a large frying pan and fry the onion for 5 minutes, until softened but not brown. Add the garlic and potatoes and cook for a few minutes, stirring occasionally.

Add the stock or water, season to taste and cook for 15 minutes, until the potatoes are tender.

Mash the potatoes roughly in the cooking liquid, add the spring greens and boil, uncovered, for 10 minutes.

Add the parsley and simmer for 2–3 minutes, until heated through. Serve with croûtons.

COOK'S NOTES This is a traditional Italian country soup. Vegetable stock will add more depth of flavour than water, but it is still delicious made with water. Serve with chunks of rosemary focaccia for a filling lunch or supper.

Preparation time:	**150 ml (6 fl oz) extra virgin olive oil**
20 minutes, plus	**1 onion, finely chopped**
soaking and chilling	**1 carrot, chopped**
	1 celery stick, chopped
Cooking time:	**2 leeks, trimmed and finely chopped**
about 3 hours	**4 garlic cloves, finely chopped**
	1 small white cabbage, shredded
Serves: **8–10**	**1 large potato, chopped**
	4 courgettes, chopped
	200 g (7 oz) dried cannellini beans,
	soaked overnight, drained and rinsed
	400 ml (14 fl oz) tomato juice or passata
	2 rosemary sprigs
	2 thyme sprigs
	2 sage sprigs
	1 dried red chilli
	2 litres (3½ pints) water
	6 large handfuls of cavolo nero or Savoy
	cabbage, finely shredded
	salt and pepper
	freshly grated Parmesan, to serve

Heat half the oil in a saucepan. Add the onion, carrot and celery and cook gently for about 10 minutes, stirring frequently. Add the leeks and garlic and cook for a further 10 minutes. Add the white cabbage, potato and courgettes and cook for a further 10 minutes, stirring frequently.

Stir in the beans, tomato juice or passata, rosemary, thyme, sage, dried red chilli, salt and plenty of pepper. Cover with the water and bring to the boil. Reduce the heat, cover the pan and simmer for at least 2 hours, until the beans are very soft.

Remove 2–3 ladlefuls of soup, purée it in a blender or food processor or rub it through a sieve and return it to the soup. Stir in the cabbage and simmer for another 15 minutes. Leave to cool and refrigerate overnight.

The next day, slowly reheat the soup and stir in the remaining olive oil. Serve with freshly grated Parmesan.

Preparation time:	**250 g (8 oz) carrots, diced**
15 minutes	**250 g (8 oz) courgettes, sliced**
	2 large celery sticks, chopped
Cooking time:	**1 large onion, finely chopped**
about 25 minutes	**125 g (4 oz) cabbage, shredded**
	600 ml (1 pint) Chicken Stock (see
Serves: **4**	**introduction)**
	300 ml (½ pint) tomato juice
	1 garlic clove, crushed
	125 g (4 oz) small pasta shapes
	salt and pepper

Place all the vegetables in a saucepan with the stock, tomato juice and garlic. Bring to the boil, reduce the heat and skim off the scum that rises to the surface.

Add the pasta, season to taste, cover the pan and simmer for 15–20 minutes or until all the vegetables and the pasta are tender. Ladle into individual bowls and serve piping hot.

COOK'S NOTES Buy special soup pasta for this soup if possible. These are usually tiny shell or pipe shapes. If you can't get soup pasta, break some spaghetti into short lengths and use that instead.

Preparation time: **5 minutes**	**2 teaspoons olive oil**
	2 celery sticks with their leaves, chopped
Cooking time: **about 40 minutes**	**2 leeks, chopped**
	1 carrot, finely diced
	50 g (2 oz) pearl barley
Serves: **4**	**1.2 litres (2 pints) Vegetable Stock (see introduction)**
	125 g (4 oz) mangetout, sliced diagonally
	salt and pepper

Heat the oil in a saucepan and add the celery, leeks and carrot. Cook over a medium heat for 10 minutes.

Stir in the pearl barley and stock, season to taste and simmer for 20 minutes. Add the mangetout and simmer for 10 minutes.

Ladle into warmed soup bowls and serve piping hot.

Preparation time: **15 minutes**	**25 g (1 oz) butter or margarine**
	1 large onion, chopped
	1 small red pepper, cored, deseeded and diced
Cooking time: **about 30 minutes**	**625 g (1¼ lb) potatoes, diced**
	25 g (1 oz) plain flour
Serves: **4–6**	**750 ml (1¼ pints) Chicken Stock (see introduction)**
	175 g (6 oz) sweetcorn kernels
	250 g (8 oz) cooked chicken, chopped
	450 ml (¾ pint) milk
	3 tablespoons chopped parsley
	salt and pepper
	red chillies, sliced, to garnish

Melt the butter or margarine in a large saucepan. Add the onion, red pepper and potatoes and fry over a moderate heat for 5 minutes, stirring from time to time.

Sprinkle in the flour and cook over a gentle heat for 1 minute. Gradually stir in the stock and bring to the boil, stirring. Lower the heat, cover the pan and cook for 10 minutes.

Stir in the sweetcorn, chicken, milk and parsley. Season to taste, cover the pan and simmer gently for a further 10 minutes until the potatoes are just tender. Taste and adjust the seasoning if necessary.

Serve the chowder garnished with the sliced chillies.

23 Chicken and coconut milk soup

24 Rice noodle soup

Preparation time: **6 minutes**	**600 ml (1 pint) Chicken Stock (see introduction)**
	6 kaffir lime leaves, torn, or ¼ teaspoon grated lime rind
Cooking time: **10 minutes**	**1 lemon grass stalk, sliced diagonally, or ¼ teaspoon grated lemon rind**
Serves: **4**	**5 cm (2 inches) galangal or fresh root ginger, peeled and finely sliced**
	200 ml (7 fl oz) coconut milk
	8 tablespoons Thai fish sauce
	2 teaspoons palm sugar or soft brown sugar
	6 tablespoons lime juice
	250 g (8 oz) boneless chicken, skinned and cut into small pieces
	4 tablespoons chilli oil or 4 small chillies, finely sliced (optional)

Heat the stock in a saucepan and add the lime leaves or rind, lemon grass or rind, and galangal or ginger. Stir to mix well and, as the stock is simmering, add the coconut milk, fish sauce, sugar and lime juice. Stir thoroughly, add the chicken pieces and simmer for 5 minutes.

Just before serving add the chilli oil or chillies, if liked, stir and serve.

Preparation time: **10 minutes, plus soaking**	**750 ml (1¼ pints) Vegetable Stock (see introduction)**
	3 spring onions, cut into 2.5 cm (1 inch) lengths
Cooking time: **8 minutes**	**2 baby corns, sliced obliquely**
	1 tomato, quartered
Serves: **4**	**1 onion, cut into 8 pieces**
	6 kaffir lime leaves, shredded
	1 celery stick, chopped
	125 g (4 oz) ready-steamed tofu, diced
	1 tablespoon soy sauce
	1 teaspoon black pepper
	1–2 teaspoons crushed dried chillies
	175 g (6 oz) dried wide rice noodles, soaked and drained
	fresh coriander leaves, cut into strips, to garnish
	lime quarters, to serve

Heat the stock in a saucepan and add all the ingredients except the rice noodles. Bring to the boil for 30 seconds, lower the heat to a simmer and cook for 5 minutes.

Add the noodles and simmer for another 2 minutes.

Pour into a serving bowl, garnish with coriander sprigs and serve with lime quarters for squeezing.

COOK'S NOTES Coconut milk is available in cans from some supermarkets and from specialist food shops. Once the can is opened, the milk will keep for only a few days in a refrigerator.

COOK'S NOTES Lime leaves give food an intense lemon aroma. They can be bought dried, when half the quantity stated should be used, or fresh, when they will keep for several weeks in the refrigerator.

2 Snacks and Starters

25 Hummus

26 Smoked mackerel pâté

Preparation time: **20 minutes, plus soaking and cooling**	**250 g (8 oz) dried chickpeas, soaked overnight, drained and rinsed**
	2–3 garlic cloves, crushed with a little salt
Cooking time: **1–1½ hours**	**about 250 ml (8 fl oz) lemon juice**
	about 5 tablespoons tahini paste
	salt
Serves: **6**	**warm pitta bread, to serve**

TO GARNISH:
extra virgin olive oil
paprika
olives

Cook the chickpeas in a large saucepan of boiling water until soft; this will take between 1 and 1½ hours, depending on their quality and age. Drain and reserve the cooking liquid. Purée the chickpeas in a blender or food processor with a little of the cooking liquid, then press the purée through a sieve to remove the skins.

Beat the garlic into the chickpea purée. Stir in the lemon juice and tahini alternately, tasting before it has all been added to get the right balance of flavours. Add a little more salt if necessary and more of the cooking liquid to make a soft, creamy consistency. Spoon the purée into a shallow dish, cover and leave in the refrigerator for several hours.

Return to room temperature before serving. Create swirls in the surface with the back of a spoon then trickle olive oil into the swirls and sprinkle lightly with paprika. Garnish with olives and serve with warm pitta bread for dipping.

Preparation time: **10 minutes**	**500 g (1 lb) smoked mackerel fillets, skinned, boned and flaked**
	1 large garlic clove, crushed
Serves: **8**	**juice of 1 lemon**
	125 g (4 oz) unsalted butter, softened
	175 g (6 oz) full-fat soft cheese
	1 tablespoon grated horseradish (fresh if available)
	black pepper

TO SERVE:
thin slices of brown bread, toasted
lemon wedges
salad leaves

Put the flaked fish in a bowl with the garlic and lemon juice. Mash well with a fork until the mackerel is finely broken up.

Work in the softened butter a little at a time. Mix in the cheese to make a smooth, well-blended mixture. Add horseradish and black pepper to taste.

Serve on thin slices of toasted brown bread, with lemon wedges and salad leaves.

COOK'S NOTES You will get a more subtle and delicious flavour if you use smoked mackerel taken from a whole smoked fish, rather than smoked fillets.

27 Carrot and coriander pâté

28 Marinated goats' cheese

Preparation time: **5 minutes, plus chilling**	**500 g (1 lb) carrots, grated**
	1 tablespoon ground coriander
	175 ml (6 fl oz) freshly squeezed orange juice
Cooking time: **20 minutes**	**300 ml (½ pint) water**
	50 g (2 oz) medium-fat soft cheese
	30 g (1¼ oz) fresh coriander leaves
Serves: **4**	**salt and pepper**
	crusty bread, to serve

Place the grated carrot in a saucepan with the ground coriander, orange juice and water. Cover the pan and simmer for 20 minutes until the carrots are cooked. Drain, cool and transfer to a blender or food processor with a little of the cooking liquid.

Add the soft cheese and coriander leaves and blend until smooth. Season to taste and blend again. Spoon into small dishes and chill before serving with crusty bread.

COOK'S NOTES Add just enough cooking liquid to make a smooth paste with the carrots. If the pâté seems too dry after you have added the cheese, add a little more cooking liquid and blend again.

Preparation time: **15 minutes, plus marinating**	**1 teaspoon fennel seeds**
	1 teaspoon pink peppercorns
	250 g (8 oz) goats' cheese, such as Saint Maure
Cooking time: **5 minutes**	**2 garlic cloves, peeled but left whole**
	2 small green chillies, bruised
	2 sprigs rosemary, bruised
Serves: **8**	**2 bay leaves, bruised**
	olive oil, to cover
	baguette, to serve

Place the fennel seeds and peppercorns in a small, heavy-based frying pan and heat gently until they start to pop and release an aroma. Leave to cool completely.

Roll the cheese into small balls and place in a bowl or jar. Add the cooled fennel seeds and peppercorns, then add the remaining ingredients with sufficient olive oil to cover.

Store in a cool place for at least 3 days, but no longer than 1 week. Serve the cheese balls with a little of the oil and chunks of baguette, or spread onto slices of toasted baguette.

COOK'S NOTES The tiny oval seeds of the fennel plant have a liquorice-like flavour, which goes particularly well with sausages, fish soup and, as here, cheese. Toasting helps bring out their flavour. To bruise an ingredient is to partially crush it in order to release its flavour.

Preparation time: **10 minutes**	**12 small new potatoes, scrubbed** **12 very thin slices of Parma ham** **2 tablespoons olive oil**
Cooking time: **30–35 minutes**	**sea salt, to serve**
Oven temperature: **200°C (400°F)** **Gas Mark 6**	
Serves: **4–6**	

Cook the potatoes in a large saucepan of boiling water for 10–15 minutes or until tender. Drain well and allow to cool.

Roll each cold cooked potato in a slice of Parma ham, patting with your hands to mould the ham to the shape of the potato.

Brush a roasting tin with the oil. Add the ham-wrapped potatoes and cook in a preheated oven, 200°C (400°F), Gas Mark 6, for 20 minutes. Serve the potatoes sprinkled with sea salt.

Preparation time: **5 minutes**	**4 large, evenly sized potatoes** **4–6 tablespoons olive oil** **½ teaspoon salt**
Cooking time: **about 1 hour**	**1–2 teaspoons chilli powder, or to taste** **soured cream, mayonnaise or aïoli,** **to serve**
Oven temperature: **220°C (425°F)** **Gas Mark 7**	
Serves: **4–6**	

Cut each potato into eight wedges and place them in a large bowl. Add the olive oil, salt and chilli powder and toss until evenly coated.

Transfer to a baking sheet and cook in a preheated oven, 220°C (425°F), Gas Mark 7, for 15 minutes. Turn the potatoes and cook for a further 15 minutes, then turn once more and cook for a final 25–30 minutes, until they are evenly crisp and golden.

Allow to cool slightly before serving with soured cream, mayonnaise or aïoli for dipping.

COOK'S NOTES **Keep an eye on the potatoes while they are cooking because they may need turning or moving – often the ones at the edges get more colour than those in the centre.**

COOK'S NOTES **To make your own quick aïoli, whisk 2 crushed garlic cloves and 3 tablespoons of extra virgin olive oil into 6 tablespoons of shop-bought mayonnaise. Chill for 2 hours before serving.**

Preparation time:	**500 g (1 lb) courgettes, grated**
10 minutes	**1 egg, beaten**
	2 tablespoons plain flour
Cooking time:	**1 chilli, deseeded and chopped**
30 minutes	**1 garlic clove, crushed**
	75 g (3 oz) Cheddar cheese, grated
Makes:	**salt and pepper**
about 12	**dill sprigs, to garnish**

TO SERVE:
smoked salmon
cream cheese

Preparation time:	**125 g (4 oz) frozen broad beans, defrosted**
10 minutes, plus	**2 tablespoons Greek yogurt**
chilling	**1 tablespoon tahini paste**
	1 tablespoon lemon juice
Cooking time:	**1 garlic clove, crushed**
10 minutes	**1 teaspoon ground coriander**
	½ teaspoon ground cumin
Serves: **4–6**	**½ teaspoon cayenne pepper**
	1 tablespoon chopped fresh coriander
	1 tablespoon chopped mint
	oil, for shallow-frying
	salt and pepper
	Greek yogurt with shredded mint leaves,
	to serve

Heat a griddle pan until hot. Meanwhile, squeeze the excess moisture out of the grated courgettes; the easiest way to do this is to place all the courgettes in a clean tea towel and squeeze well.

Mix together the egg and flour until smooth. Add all the other ingredients, mix well and season to taste.

Place spoonfuls of the mixture on to the griddle, flatten with a palette knife and allow the fritters to cook for 4–5 minutes. Turn and cook for a further 4–5 minutes. Do not disturb them while they are cooking because a crust needs to form on the cooking side, otherwise the fritter will be difficult to turn.

Keep the cooked fritters warm and repeat until all the mixture has been used. Serve the fritters garnished with sprigs of dill and between layers of smoked salmon and cream cheese.

Drain the broad beans and dry thoroughly. Place in a blender or food processor and blend to form a fairly smooth paste. Transfer the puréed beans to a bowl. Stir in all the remaining ingredients, except the oil, and season to taste. Cover and chill for 1 hour.

Form the mixture into small patties. Heat a little oil in a frying pan and fry the patties, a few at a time, for 1–2 minutes on each side until golden-brown.

Drain on kitchen paper and keep warm while frying the remaining patties. Serve hot with mint-flavoured yogurt.

COOK'S NOTES Tahini is an oily paste made of ground, raw sesame seeds. It is often used in Middle Eastern cooking. Stir well before using because it tends to separate when left standing.

33 Stuffed vine leaves

34 Mexican stuffed peppers

Preparation time:	**2 teaspoons vegetable oil**
30 minutes	**1 onion, chopped**
	1 garlic clove, crushed
Cooking time:	**75 g (3 oz) chicken livers**
30–40 minutes	**125 g (4 oz) cooked rice**
	25 g (1 oz) pine nuts
Oven temperature:	**36 canned vine leaves**
180°C (350°F)	**about 300 ml (½ pint) Chicken Stock (see**
Gas Mark 4	**introduction)**
	salt and pepper
Serves: **6–8**	

Heat the oil in a frying pan and fry the onion and garlic until soft and transparent. Add the chicken livers and fry for a further 3 minutes, stirring constantly, until browned on all sides. Remove the livers from the pan and chop finely. Place the rice in a bowl and add the chopped liver, onion, garlic and pan juices and the pine nuts. Season to taste and mix well.

Lay the vine leaves on a large board or work surface with the underside of the leaves uppermost. Put a teaspoon of the rice mixture on each leaf and roll them up, tucking the sides in, to make neat parcels. Place the leaves close together in a casserole, making two or more layers.

Pour in enough stock to come halfway up the sides of the casserole and just cover the vine leaves. Cover and place in a preheated oven, 180°C (350°F), Gas Mark 4, for 30–40 minutes until cooked through. Serve at once, or leave until cold.

COOK'S NOTES To make vegetarian stuffed vine leaves, replace the chicken livers with 25 g (1 oz) of raisins and use 175 g (6 oz) of cooked rice. Cook the parcels in Vegetable Stock (see introduction).

Preparation time:	**6 large green peppers**
30 minutes	**2 eggs, separated**
	flour, for coating
Cooking time:	**oil, for frying**
35–40 minutes	**salt and pepper**
Serves: **6**	PICADILLO:
	1–2 tablespoons vegetable oil
	750 g (1½ lb) lean minced beef
	1 large onion, chopped
	1 garlic clove, crushed
	2 large cooking apples, peeled, cored
	** and finely chopped**
	200 g (7 oz) can chopped tomatoes
	15 g (½ oz) pimento–stuffed olives, sliced
	25 g (1 oz) raisins
	15 g (½ oz) chillies, sliced
	large pinch each of cinnamon and cloves
	salt and pepper

First make the picadillo. Heat the oil in a frying pan, brown the meat and add the onion, garlic and apple. Cook for about 10 minutes, then drain to remove any fat. Add the rest of the ingredients and season to taste. Continue to cook until the mixture is rather dry.

Make a long slit in the side of each pepper and carefully scoop out the seeds without tearing the skin. Stuff each one with picadillo mixture.

Beat the egg whites in a bowl until they form stiff peaks. In a separate bowl beat the egg yolks and salt and pepper until pale, then gently fold in the beaten egg white. Dip the stuffed peppers in the flour and then into the egg mixture. Heat 1 cm (½ inch) of oil in a large frying pan, and fry the peppers in batches over a low heat, turning occasionally, until they are uniformly golden all over and the filling is sealed inside the egg coating. Drain on kitchen paper, slice and serve.

35 Stuffed vegetables with couscous

36 Thai egg strips

Preparation time:	**2 beefsteak tomatoes**
15 minutes	**2 red, orange or yellow peppers**
	2 tablespoons olive oil
Cooking time:	**175 g (6 oz) couscous**
30 minutes	**300 ml (½ pint) boiling water**
	½ bunch of spring onions, chopped
Oven temperature:	**small handful of basil leaves, torn**
200°C (400°F)	**into pieces**
Gas Mark 6	**125 g (4 oz) mozzarella, drained and**
	chopped
Serves: **4**	**25 g (1 oz) Parmesan, freshly grated**
	400 g (13 oz) can chickpeas, rinsed
	and drained
	salt and pepper

Halve the tomatoes horizontally and scoop out the seeds. Halve the peppers lengthways and discard the core and seeds. Put the tomatoes and peppers, cut sides up, in a large, shallow, ovenproof dish and drizzle with the oil and a little salt and pepper. Bake in a preheated oven, 200°C (400 °F), Gas Mark 6, for 20 minutes until softened.

Meanwhile, put the couscous in a bowl, pour on the boiling water and leave to stand for 10 minutes until the water is absorbed. Fluff up the couscous with a fork and stir in the spring onions, basil, mozzarella, Parmesan and chickpeas. Season to taste.

Spoon the couscous mixture into the baked vegetables and return the dish to the oven for a further 8–10 minutes until the vegetables have heated through and the mozzarella has melted. Serve warm.

COOK'S NOTES Chickpeas add texture and flavour but they can be left out altogether or replaced with a sprinkling of toasted pine nuts if preferred. Parmesan adds plenty of flavour, but grated mature Cheddar can be substituted.

Preparation time:	**3 eggs, beaten**
5 minutes	**1 shallot, finely sliced**
	green shoots of 1 spring onion, sliced
Cooking time:	**1–2 small red chillies, finely chopped**
2–3 minutes	**1 tablespoon chopped fresh coriander**
	leaves
Serves: **2**	**1 tablespoon groundnut oil**
	salt and pepper
	julienne strips of spring onion, to garnish
	(optional)

Mix all the ingredients, except the oil, in a bowl. Season to taste with salt and pepper.

Heat the oil in a frying pan or wok, pour in the egg mixture and swirl it around the pan to produce a large, thin omelette. Cook for 1–2 minutes until firm.

Slide the omelette on to a plate and roll it up as if it were a pancake. Allow to cool.

When the omelette is cool, cut the roll crossways into 5 mm (¼ inch) or 1 cm (½ inch) sections, depending on how wide you want the strips to be. Serve them rolled up or straightened out in a heap, garnished with strips of spring onion, if liked.

Preparation time:	**5 g (¼ oz) butter**
5 minutes	**1 small red onion, sliced into rings**
	1 egg, beaten
Cooking time:	**2 slices of smoked salmon**
5 minutes	**2 slices of crusty bread or pumpernickel, buttered**
Serves: **1**	**salt and pepper**

TO SERVE:

capers

cornichons

pickled onions

Melt the butter in a nonstick saucepan. Gently fry the onion rings for 1–2 minutes until they are just soft. Remove them from the pan and set aside. Season the egg and add to the pan. Stir with a wooden spoon over a gentle heat until the mixture becomes thick and creamy.

Place the salmon slices on top of the slices of bread. Top with the lightly scrambled egg and the onion rings. Serve with capers, cornichons and pickled onions.

COOK'S NOTES Remove the pan from the heat just before the egg is cooked to the desired consistency as it will continue to cook in its own heat for a short while afterwards.

Preparation time:	**1 ciabatta loaf or baguette**
20 minutes	**3–4 tablespoons extra virgin olive oil**
	12 anchovy fillets, sliced, to serve
Cooking time:	**6 basil leaves, to garnish**
6 minutes	
	PESTO:
Oven temperature:	**1–2 handfuls basil leaves**
200°C (400°F)	**1–2 garlic cloves**
Gas mark 6	**2 tablespoons pine nuts, lightly toasted**
	2 tablespoons finely grated Parmesan
Makes: **6**	**1 tablespoon finely grated pecorino**
	100 ml (3½ fl oz) virgin olive oil
	salt and pepper

TOPPING:

50 g (2 oz) pitted black olives, chopped

2 tomatoes, diced

½ small onion, chopped

1 garlic clove, crushed

½ tablespoon chopped parsley

½ tablespoon chopped basil

First make the pesto. Put the basil, garlic, pine nuts and a pinch of salt in a mortar and grind with a pestle to make a paste. Alternatively, use a blender or food processor. Add the cheeses and mix thoroughly. Slowly pour in the oil, stirring well with a wooden spoon. Season to taste.

Next make the topping. Mix together the olives, tomatoes, onion, garlic and herbs. Season to taste.

Cut the bread into slices at an angle and arrange them on a baking sheet, lightly greased with some of the olive oil. Drizzle the remaining oil over the bread. Bake in a preheated oven, 200°C (400°F), Gas Mark 6, for 5–6 minutes, turning once.

Spread some pesto on each piece of bread then spoon over the topping. Arrange two anchovies on each slice and garnish with basil leaves.

39 Bruschetta with peppers

Preparation time: 10 minutes

Cooking time: 15 minutes

Serves: 4

4 red peppers
1 rosemary sprig, finely chopped
125 g (4 oz) Parmesan shavings
1–2 tablespoons olive oil
4 large, thick slices of crusty bread
2 garlic cloves
salt and pepper
rosemary leaves, to garnish

Heat a griddle pan until hot and griddle all the peppers until the skin is charred all over. Peel the skin from the peppers and roughly chop the flesh. Add the rosemary and half the Parmesan shavings. Season to taste and mix well with a little olive oil.

Toast or griddle the bread on both sides. Rub one side of the bread with the garlic cloves and drizzle over the remaining olive oil.

Heat the grill. Place the prepared toast on a baking sheet, spoon the pepper mix on to the bread and spread evenly. Sprinkle with the remaining Parmesan shavings and place under the grill for a few minutes or until sizzling.

Serve garnished with the rosemary leaves.

40 Quesadillas

Preparation time: 15 minutes

Cooking time: 5–10 minutes per batch

Serves: 6

12 soft corn tortillas
175 g (6 oz) canned refried beans
250 g (8 oz) Cheddar, grated
125 g (4 oz) mozzarella, cut into strips
4–6 green chillies, deseeded and thinly sliced
oil, for frying

TO SERVE:
Salsa Cruda (see Cook's Notes below)
guacamole
soured cream

Put the tortillas on a board and divide the refried beans among them, spreading a spoonful of the mixture on one half of each tortilla and leaving a little space around the edge.

Put a little Cheddar and some mozzarella on top of the beans and then add a few slices of chilli. Fold the tortillas over the filling.

Press the edges of each folded tortilla firmly between your fingertips. It helps if the tortillas are soft and quite damp when you do this. If necessary, secure them with cocktail sticks. Cover the folded tortillas with a damp cloth while you make the remaining quesadillas.

Add some oil to a large pan to a depth of 4 cm (1½ inches). Heat the oil and fry the quesadillas in batches until they are crisp and golden-brown. Remove and drain on kitchen paper. Serve hot with the salsa, guacamole and soured cream.

COOK'S NOTES To make Salsa Cruda, put 500 g (1 lb) tomatoes, skinned and chopped, 2 green chillies, deseeded and finely chopped and 1 onion, finely chopped, in a bowl with a pinch of sugar. Season to taste and add some chopped coriander. Mix together before serving.

41 Focaccia sandwich

Preparation time: **10 minutes**

Cooking time: **20 minutes**

Serves: **4**

1 small aubergine, sliced
2 courgettes, sliced lengthways
1 red onion, sliced into rings
1 loaf of focaccia bread
1 garlic clove, halved (optional)
1 packet of mozzarella, sliced
2 red peppers, griddled and skinned
75 g (3 oz) rocket
olive oil, to drizzle
salt and pepper

Heat the griddle pan and griddle the aubergine, courgettes and red onion for about 5 minutes, turning occasionally. Leave to cool.

Cut the focaccia in half lengthways and place it on the griddle to toast lightly. Rub the cut garlic edges all over the toasted bread if wished.

Place the sliced mozzarella on the base of the toasted focaccia then evenly layer the griddled vegetables on top of the mozzarella. Start with the aubergine and then add the courgettes, peppers, onion and rocket. Season each layer as you arrange it.

Finally, drizzle with a little olive oil, season and place the top of the focaccia bread on top of the vegetables. Push together gently but firmly. Cut into four evenly sized pieces and serve.

COOK'S NOTES Ready roasted or griddled red pepper slices or halves can be found in delicatessens or in jars in supermarkets, usually preserved in oil.

42 Great steak sandwich

Preparation time: **20 minutes**

Cooking time: **about 40 minutes**

Serves: **4**

5 tablespoons olive oil
2 teaspoons mustard seeds
2 large red onions, finely sliced
2 garlic cloves, crushed
1 tablespoon chopped flat leaf parsley
1 tablespoon balsamic vinegar
4 sirloin seaks, 125–150 g (4–5 oz) each
1 tablespoon crushed black peppercorns
8 large slices of olive bread or other crusty bread
2 ripe beefsteak tomatoes, sliced
75 g (3 oz) fontina or Gruyère, thinly sliced
125 g (4 oz) rocket
salt and pepper

Heat 4 tablespoons of the olive oil in a medium frying pan, add the mustard seeds, cover and let them pop for 30 seconds over a moderate heat; take care that they do not burn. Add the onions and garlic, cover and cook over a very low heat for 30 minutes, until they are very soft but not coloured.

Purée the softened onion mixture in a blender or food processor, then spoon into a bowl. Stir in the parsley and vinegar. Season to taste, cover and set aside.

Brush the steaks with a little of the remaining oil. Press the crushed black peppercorns into both sides. Place the steaks under a preheated medium-hot grill. Cook for 4–5 minutes on each side for medium-rare or 5–6 minutes for medium.

Toast the bread slices on both sides until lightly golden. Spread 4 slices with the onion purée and cover with slices of tomato. Add a piece of steak to each and top with the cheese slices and rocket. Season, cover with the remaining toasted bread slices and serve at once.

43 Club sandwich

Preparation time: **about 10 minutes**	**6 back bacon rashers**
	6 slices of bread
	6 tablespoons mayonnaise
Cooking time: **5–7 minutes**	**8 lettuce leaves**
	2 large slices of cooked turkey
	2 tomatoes, thinly sliced
Serves: **2**	**salt and pepper**

Cook the bacon in a large frying pan for 5–7 minutes, turning once, until crisp on both sides. Remove and drain on kitchen paper.

Meanwhile, toast the bread on both sides. Place the toast on a large board or work surface and spread one side of each slice with a tablespoon of mayonnaise.

Arrange two lettuce leaves on each of two slices of toast and season with salt and pepper to taste. Arrange one slice of turkey on top of the lettuce on each sandwich base, then top with another slice of toast, mayonnaise side up. Arrange the remaining lettuce leaves on top and add the tomato slices, then the crisp bacon, cutting the rashers to fit as necessary.

Cover with the remaining two slices of toast, mayonnaise side down. Leave the sandwiches whole, or cut them into four triangles and pierce with long toothpicks. Serve immediately.

44 Sausage and bacon rolls

Preparation time: **15 minutes**	**8 bacon rashers**
	1–2 teaspoons Dijon mustard
	4 large sausages (beef or pork)
Cooking time: **10 minutes**	**8 large sage leaves**
	2 tablespoons vegetable oil
	4 long country bread rolls or frankfurter
Serves: **4**	**rolls**
	25 g (1 oz) butter, softened
	relishes, to serve

Stretch each bacon rasher with the back of a knife and spread one side of each with a little mustard. Wrap 2 rashers around each sausage so that the mustard is on the inside. Tuck the sage leaves under the bacon and secure with toothpicks.

Heat the oil in a large frying pan. Add the wrapped sausages and cook for 10 minutes over a moderately high heat, shaking the pan occasionally, until the bacon is browned on both sides.

Split the rolls in half lengthways and toast lightly. Spread the cut surfaces with butter and a little mustard, if liked. Remove the toothpicks and place one sausage in each roll.

Serve at once with a selection of relishes.

COOK'S NOTES Remember the sausages will take longer to cook than usual with the bacon wrapped around them. Ensure they are cooked through before serving.

3 Vegetables and Salads

45 Scalloped potatoes

46 Potatoes dauphinoise

Preparation time:
20 minutes

Cooking time:
1 hour 20 minutes

Oven temperature:
180°C (350°F)
Gas Mark 4

Serves: **6**

2 teaspoons vegetable oil
75 ml (3 fl oz) soured cream
350 ml (12 fl oz) milk
25 g (1 oz) butter
1 tablespoon cornflour
4 medium potatoes, about 750 g (1½ lb),
**   cut into 5 mm (¼ inch) slices**
½ onion, chopped
pinch of paprika
pepper
thyme sprigs, to serve

Preparation time:
15 minutes

Cooking time:
1–1¼ hours

Oven temperature:
180°C (350°F)
Gas Mark 4;
then 200°C (400°F)
Gas Mark 6

Serves: **2–3**

500 g (1 lb) potatoes, thinly sliced
40 g (1½ oz) butter
1 large garlic clove, crushed
300 ml (½ pint) double cream
salt and pepper
red and green chillies, finely sliced, to
**   garnish (optional)**
French beans, to serve

Brush a rectangular baking dish, 20 x 12 cm (8 x 5 inches), with oil.

Whisk together the soured cream, milk, butter, cornflour and pepper.

Line the dish with one-third of the potato slices. Pour one-third of the soured cream mixture over the potatoes. Sprinkle half of the onion over the soured cream mixture. Repeat the layers, adding another third of the potatoes, another third of the soured cream mixture and the remaining onion. Arrange the remaining potatoes on the top and pour the remaining soured cream mixture over the top. Cover with foil and bake in a preheated oven, 180°C (350°F), Gas Mark 4, for 1 hour. Remove the foil and bake for a further 20 minutes.

Sprinkle with paprika and thyme sprigs. Allow to stand for about 5 minutes before serving.

Wash the sliced potatoes and pat dry with kitchen paper. Butter an ovenproof dish, scatter with crushed garlic and fill with layers of the potato slices.

Pour over the cream and sprinkle with salt and black pepper. Bake the dish in a preheated oven, 180°C (350°F), Gas Mark 4, for 1–1¼ hours or until the potatoes are tender when pierced with a skewer.

Increase the heat to 200°C (400°F), Gas Mark 6, for the last 10 minutes to brown the top. Garnish with the chillies, if using, and serve hot on a bed of French beans.

COOK'S NOTES If you are counting the calories, use low-fat soured cream, skimmed milk and low-fat spread in place of the full-fat ingredients in this recipe.

Preparation time:
10 minutes

Cooking time:
25–30 minutes

Oven temperature:
230°C (450°F)
Gas Mark 8

Serves: **4**

750 g (1½ lb) potatoes, scrubbed
4 tablespoons olive oil
2 tablespoons chopped rosemary
4 garlic cloves, sliced
salt and pepper
rosemary sprig, to garnish

Cut the potatoes lengthways into quarters and pat dry with kitchen paper. Put 2 tablespoons of the olive oil in a large roasting tin and place in a preheated oven, 230°C (450°F), Gas Mark 8, to warm through.

Mix together the remaining oil and the rosemary in a large bowl and toss the potatoes in the oil until they are completely coated.

Add the potatoes to the roasting tin in the oven, shake carefully so that the potatoes are in an even layer, then place the tin at the top of the oven and roast for 20 minutes.

Remove the tin from the oven and move the potatoes around so that they cook evenly. Scatter the garlic among the potatoes, return the tin to the oven and cook for a further 5 minutes. Remove the potatoes from the oven, season, garnish with a sprig of rosemary and serve immediately while still very hot.

Preparation time:
5–10 minutes

Cooking time:
about 30 minutes

Serves: **4**

1 kg (2 lb) evenly sized floury potatoes,
scrubbed but unpeeled
75 g (3 oz) butter
1 small mild onion, finely chopped
salt and pepper

Cook the potatoes in a large saucepan of lightly salted boiling water for about 7 minutes. Drain well. When the potatoes are quite cold, peel them and grate them coarsely into a bowl.

Heat 15 g (½ oz) of the butter in a large frying pan. Add the onion and cook for about 5 minutes until it is soft. Stir the onion into the grated potato and season to taste.

Melt the remaining butter in the frying pan. Set aside about 1 tablespoon of the melted butter in a cup. Add the potato mixture to the pan and form it into a neat cake. Cook gently for about 15 minutes, shaking the pan occasionally so that the rösti cake does not stick, until the underside of the cake is a crusty golden-brown.

To cook the top of the rösti, pour over the reserved melted butter and either place the frying pan under a preheated grill to brown or turn the rösti over in the pan and brown.

To serve invert the rösti cake on a warmed flat dish and cut it into wedges.

COOK'S NOTES This potato cake can be flavoured with many different herbs and spices. Try chopped thyme, sage or rosemary, cumin or caraway seeds, or a pinch of paprika or chilli powder.

Preparation time:	**75 g (3 oz) butter or margarine**
10 minutes	**750 g (1½ lb) cooked potatoes, fairly thickly sliced**
Cooking time:	**sea salt**
10 minutes	**chopped thyme, to garnish**

Serves: **4**

Heat the butter or margarine in a large frying pan. Add the potatoes and sauté gently for about 10 minutes, turning them often until the slices are golden-brown on both sides. Sprinkle with sea salt and thyme just before serving.

Preparation time:	**500 g (1 lb) pink new potatoes or blue truffle potatoes, halved**
5 minutes	**2 fennel heads, cut into thin wedges**
Cooking time:	**olive oil, to drizzle**
30 minutes	**salt and pepper**

Serves: **4**

Heat a griddle pan until hot. Griddle the first batch of potatoes for 10 minutes on each side or until they are soft when tested with a knife. Remove the potatoes from the heat and keep them warm, allowing them to sit for 10 minutes to steam in their skins while you griddle the rest of the potatoes.

Griddle the fennel for 3–4 minutes on each side. Add to the cooked potatoes, drizzle with olive oil and season well.

51 Spinach with lemon dressing

52 Grilled courgettes with mustard

Preparation time: **about 10 minutes**

Cooking time: **5 minutes**

Serves: **6**

625 g (1¼ lb) spinach
2 tablespoons butter
2 garlic cloves, finely chopped
4 tablespoons olive oil
2 tablespoons lemon juice
salt and pepper
shredded lemon rind, to garnish

Preparation time: **10 minutes**

Cooking time: **10 minutes**

Serves: **4**

500 g (1 lb) courgettes, halved
lengthways
15 g (½ oz) butter or margarine, melted
1 tablespoon wholegrain mustard

Wash the spinach in a colander and shake off the excess water, then put it in a large saucepan. Sprinkle the spinach with salt to taste. Cover the pan and cook over a moderate heat for 1–2 minutes, shaking the pan vigorously from time to time, until the spinach has wilted and is tender.

Drain the spinach thoroughly in a colander, then return it to the pan and toss over a high heat until any remaining water has evaporated. Add the butter and garlic and continue tossing until they are combined with the spinach.

Turn the spinach into a serving dish. Drizzle with oil and lemon juice, season to taste and garnish with lemon rind.

Brush the courgettes lightly with the melted butter or margarine and place them, cut side down, on a grill pan. Cook under a preheated hot grill until lightly browned.

Turn over the courgettes and spread the cut sides with mustard. Grill until golden. Serve hot as a starter or an accompanying vegetable.

COOK'S NOTES Spinach is available all year round and is highly nutritious, being rich in iron and vitamins. If you use frozen spinach, defrost it thoroughly and do not add any more water.

COOK'S NOTES Soya margarine can be used instead of butter or vegetable margarine for all dishes. It is suitable for vegans and is a healthy choice because it is particularly low in saturated fats.

53 Honey carrots

54 Pan-braised peppers with tomato

Preparation time;
10 minutes

Cooking time:
12 minutes

Serves: **6**

125 ml (4 fl oz) water
750 g (1½ lb) baby carrots, fresh or frozen
1 tablespoon margarine
1 tablespoon soft light brown sugar
2 tablespoons honey
2–3 tablespoons finely chopped parsley

Pour the water into a saucepan. Add the carrots and bring to the boil. Reduce the heat, cover and simmer for about 10 minutes or until the carrots are still slightly crisp. Drain. If you are using frozen carrots, follow the directions on the packet.

Melt the margarine in a frying pan over medium-high heat. Add the sugar, honey and carrots. Reduce the heat and turn the carrots frequently for 1–2 minutes until they are well glazed. Sprinkle with parsley before serving.

Preparation time:
25 minutes

Cooking time:
8 minutes

Serves: **4**

1 tablespoon vegetable oil
2 onions, coarsely chopped
3 large peppers, red, green and yellow, total weight about 500 g (1 lb), cored, deseeded and cut into strips
500 g (1 lb) tomatoes, skinned and chopped
1 teaspoon coriander seeds
1 teaspoon black peppercorns
½ teaspoon salt
½ teaspoon ground chilli

Heat the oil in a large frying pan and fry the onions for about 5 minutes until golden. Add the peppers and cook gently for 2–3 minutes, then stir in the tomatoes.

Crush the coriander seeds and peppercorns. Use a pestle and mortar if you have one, otherwise put the seeds and peppercorns between double sheets of kitchen paper and crush them with a rolling pin. Add the salt and chilli to the crushed seeds and sprinkle the mixture over the peppers and tomatoes. Mix together lightly, cover the pan and cook gently for 20 minutes.

This dish can be prepared up to 24 hours in advance and kept, covered, in the refrigerator.

COOK'S NOTES **To skin tomatoes, place them in a bowl of boiling water and leave for 1 minute. Remove one and start to peel away the skin. If it is difficult to remove, return to the boiling water for another minute, then drain and peel them all.**

55 Leeks, asparagus and peppers

Preparation time:
10 minutes

Cooking time:
15 minutes

Serves: **4**

2 red peppers, cored, deseeded and quartered
250 g (8 oz) baby leeks
250 g (8 oz) asparagus
3 tablespoons extra virgin olive oil
2 tablespoons balsamic vinegar
1 bunch of flat leaf parsley, chopped
salt and pepper

Heat a griddle pan until hot. Place the red peppers, baby leeks and asparagus on the griddle pan and cook for 5 minutes, turning them from time to time until they are lightly charred and tender.

Mix the vegetables with the olive oil, balsamic vinegar and chopped parsley. Season to taste and serve.

56 Spicy roast vegetables

Preparation time:
10 minutes

Cooking time:
15 minutes

Serves: **6**

2 tablespoons extra virgin olive oil
½ teaspoon white cumin seeds
1 green pepper, cored, deseeded and thickly sliced
1 red pepper, cored, deseeded and thickly sliced
1 orange pepper, cored, deseeded and thickly sliced
2 courgettes, diagonally sliced
2 tomatoes, halved
2 red onions, quartered
1 aubergine, thickly sliced
2 thick fresh green chillies, sliced
4 garlic cloves
2.5 cm (1 inch) fresh root ginger, shredded
1 teaspoon dried crushed red chillies
½ teaspoon salt
1 tablespoon chopped fresh coriander, to garnish
lemon wedges, to serve

Heat a grill pan for 2 minutes. Pour in the olive oil, then add the cumin seeds. Lower the heat to medium.

Arrange the vegetables in the pan with a pair of tongs, then add the green chillies, garlic, ginger, red chillies and salt and increase the heat. Cook the vegetables for 7–10 minutes, turning them with the tongs.

Serve hot with lemon wedges and garnish with the fresh coriander.

57 Stir-fried vegetables

58 Braised okra with chillies

Preparation time:
15–20 minutes

Cooking time:
3–5 minutes

Serves: 4

1 tablespoon vegetable oil
125 g (4 oz) bamboo shoots, thinly sliced
50 g (2 oz) mangetout
125 g (4 oz) carrots, thinly sliced
50 g (2 oz) broccoli florets
125 g (4 oz) fresh bean sprouts
1 teaspoon salt
1 teaspoon sugar
1 tablespoon water

Heat the oil in a preheated frying pan or wok. Add the bamboo shoots, mangetout, carrots and broccoli florets and stir-fry for about 1 minute.

Add the bean sprouts and then the salt and sugar. Stir-fry for another minute or so, and add some water if necessary. Do not overcook or the vegetables will lose their crunchiness. Serve hot.

Preparation time:
15 minutes

Cooking time:
about 15 minutes

Serves: 4

50 g (2 oz) ghee or butter
1 large onion, sliced
3 garlic cloves, sliced
5 cm (2 inches) fresh root ginger, peeled and finely chopped
2 fresh green chillies, deseeded and finely chopped
½ teaspoon chilli powder
500 g (1 lb) okra, trimmed
200 ml (7 fl oz) water
2 teaspoons desiccated coconut
salt

Melt the ghee or butter in a large wok or saucepan. Add the onion, garlic, ginger, chillies and chilli powder and fry gently, stirring occasionally, for 4–5 minutes until soft.

Add the okra, water and salt to taste. Bring to the boil, lower the heat, cover and simmer for 5–10 minutes until the okra are just tender but still firm to the bite. Stir in the coconut and serve hot.

COOK'S NOTES It is best to use fresh bean sprouts for this dish, so buy them on the day you plan to use them. Canned bean sprouts do not have the crunchy texture that you need for this recipe.

59 Radicchio with blue cheese salad

60 Fatoush salad with fried haloumi

Preparation time:
10 minutes

Serves: **4**

1 head of radicchio, leaves separated
125 g (4 oz) Danish blue, crumbled
1 tablespoon thick mayonnaise
salt and pepper
snipped chives, to garnish

Divide the radicchio among four individual serving dishes.

Mix the blue cheese with the mayonnaise in a bowl and season to taste. Spoon the blue cheese mixture over the radicchio, dividing it equally among the dishes. Garnish with the sniped chives.

Preparation time:
30 minutes

Cooking time:
10 minutes

Serves: **4**

2 green peppers, cored, deseeded
and diced
½ cucumber, diced
4 ripe tomatoes, diced
1 red onion, finely chopped
2 garlic cloves, crushed
2 tablespoons chopped parsley
1 tablespoon each chopped mint and
coriander
2 pitta breads
4 tablespoons olive oil
125 g (4 oz) haloumi, sliced

LEMON DRESSING:
6 tablespoons extra virgin olive oil
1–2 tablespoons lemon juice
1 tablespoon water
¼ teaspoon sugar
salt and pepper

Combine the peppers, cucumber, tomatoes, onion, garlic and herbs in a large bowl.

Make the dressing by whisking together all the ingredients, season to taste, then toss with the salad until well coated.

Griddle or grill the pitta bread until it is toasted, tear it into bite-sized pieces and add to the salad. Stir well and leave to infuse for at least 20 minutes.

Heat the oil in a frying pan and fry the haloumi slices on both sides for 2–3 minutes until they are golden and softened. Serve with the salad.

COOK'S NOTES Stilton and Roquefort can also be used to good effect in this salad as they have the same intense saltiness as Danish Blue.

61 Warm goats' cheese salad

Preparation time:
15 minutes

Cooking time:
15 minutes

Oven temperature:
180°C (350°F)
Gas Mark 4

Serves: 6

6 slices of wholemeal or French bread
2 x 100 g (3½ oz) round goats' cheeses, sliced
100 g (3½ oz) mixed salad leaves, to serve

DRESSING:
1 tablespoon tarragon vinegar
3 tablespoons olive oil
½ teaspoon Dijon mustard

TO GARNISH:
25 g (1 oz) pine nuts, toasted
basil leaves

First make the dressing. Combine the vinegar, oil and mustard in a small screw-top jar. Screw on the lid tightly and shake vigorously for about a minute until well combined.

Using a biscuit cutter, cut a round out of each slice of bread or, if you are using French bread, cut slices. Place the bread on a baking sheet and cook in a preheated oven, 180°C (350°F), Gas Mark 4, for 10 minutes.

Cover each slice of bread with cheese slices. Cook the cheese under a hot grill for 5 minutes or until golden and bubbling.

Arrange beds of salad leaves on six small serving plates. Drizzle the salad leaves with the dressing and place the cheese rounds on top. Scatter the pine nuts and basil leaves over the top, before serving.

62 Greek salad with tahini dressing

Preparation time:
15–20 minutes

Serves:
4–6 as a side salad

½ large cucumber
375 g (12 oz) tomatoes, cut into thin wedges
1 small green pepper, cut into quarters, deseeded and sliced
1 small onion, finely sliced
8 small black olives, pitted and halved
125 g (4 oz) feta

TAHINI DRESSING:
2 tablespoons tahini paste
4 tablespoons natural yogurt
1–2 tablespoons water
2 tablespoons chopped parsley
1 small garlic clove
salt and pepper

Cut the cucumber into 5 mm (¼ inch) slices, then cut these across into 5 mm (¼ inch) batons. Place them in a salad bowl and add the tomatoes, green pepper, onion and olives.

Next make the dressing. Spoon the tahini paste into a small bowl. Slowly beat in the yogurt and add water as necessary to thin it down. Stir in the parsley and garlic, and salt and pepper to taste.

Pour the dressing over the salad and toss well. Cut the feta into small cubes and sprinkle over the salad.

COOK'S NOTES To toast pine nuts, place them in a dry frying pan over a medium heat and toss frequently until they are golden on all sides.

63 Mixed-leaf and bacon salad

Preparation time:
10 minutes

Cooking time:
8 minutes

Serves: **4**

2 tablespoons olive oil
8 streaky bacon rashers
1 garlic clove, finely chopped
200 g (7 oz) mixed salad leaves (such as rocket, curly endive and lollo rosso)
1 small red chilli, thinly sliced, to garnish

CLASSIC VINAIGRETTE:
5 tablespoons olive oil
2 tablespoons white wine vinegar
1 teaspoon Dijon mustard
pinch of sugar
salt and pepper

Heat 1 tablespoon of the olive oil in a frying pan and cook the bacon until it is crisp. Remove from the pan and drain on kitchen paper.

Add the second tablespoon of oil to the pan and cook the garlic for 2–3 minutes, stirring constantly. Remove the pan from the heat.

Next make the vinaigrette. Put the olive oil and vinegar in a bowl and mix with a fork. Whisk in the mustard and sugar until the mixture is thoroughly blended. Season to taste.

Cut the bacon into bite-sized pieces. Place the salad leaves in a large bowl or four individual bowls. Pour the dressing over the leaves and scatter the bacon and garlic on top. Garnish the salad with the chilli.

64 Ratatouille niçoise

Preparation time:
20 minutes

Cooking time:
about 40 minutes

Serves: **6**

125 ml (4 fl oz) olive oil
500 g (1 lb) aubergines, thinly sliced or diced
500 g (1 lb) courgettes, sliced
500 g (1 lb) onions, thinly sliced
500 g (1 lb) green peppers, cored, deseeded and thinly sliced
5 garlic cloves, crushed
750 g (1½ lb) tomatoes, skinned and roughly chopped
2 thyme sprigs
5 basil leaves
salt and pepper
chopped parsley, to garnish

Heat half of the oil in a large saucepan and add the aubergines. Fry them gently over a moderate heat, stirring frequently, until they are lightly golden.

Add the courgettes and continue frying for 5–6 minutes until they are lightly coloured. Remove the aubergines and courgettes from the pan with a slotted spoon and set aside.

Add the remaining oil to the pan. Stir in the onions and fry gently until soft and golden. Add the peppers and garlic, increase the heat and fry for 3–4 minutes. Add the chopped tomatoes and cook gently for 10 minutes. Return the aubergines and courgettes to the pan, stir, season to taste and crumble in the thyme. Cook gently, uncovered, for about 20 minutes. Crumble the basil leaves into the ratatouille, and serve it warm or cold, sprinkled with parsley.

COOK'S NOTES The quantities of the different vegetables can be varied according to your preference. You could also use red or yellow peppers as well as green to add more colour.

65 Provençal pasta salad

66 Spinach, mushroom and hazelnut salad

Preparation time:
10–12 minutes, plus cooling

Cooking time:
about 12 minutes

Serves: **6**

175 g (6 oz) rigatoni or penne
4 tablespoons low-fat mayonnaise
juice of ½ lemon
6 tomatoes, skinned, deseeded and chopped
125 g (4 oz) French beans, cooked
12 black olives, pitted
200 g (7 oz) can tuna in brine, drained and flaked
salt and pepper
50 g (2 oz) can anchovy fillets, drained and washed, to garnish
1 small lettuce, shredded, to serve

Bring a large saucepan of salted water to the boil. Add the pasta, stir and cook for 10–12 minutes or until it is tender but firm to the bite (al dente). Drain the pasta well and mix with a little of the mayonnaise.

Allow the pasta to cool, turn it into a bowl and mix with the lemon juice, tomatoes, beans, olives and flaked tuna and season to taste.

Toss the salad lightly in the remaining mayonnaise and serve on a bed of shredded lettuce, garnished with anchovies.

Preparation time:
15 minutes

Serves: **6**

2 teaspoons olive oil
2 tablespoons white wine vinegar
1 garlic clove, chopped
2 tablespoons roughly chopped parsley
3 tablespoons natural yogurt
175 g (6 oz) young fresh spinach leaves, washed and shaken
125 g (4 oz) button mushrooms, thinly sliced
25 g (1 oz) hazelnuts
salt and pepper

To make the dressing, blend together the olive oil, wine vinegar, garlic, parsley and yogurt. Season to taste and blend in a liquidizer until it is smooth.

Tear the spinach leaves into pieces and divide these among 6 individual salad plates.

Scatter the mushrooms and hazelnuts over the spinach. Spoon the prepared dressing over each serving and toss lightly.

COOK'S NOTES This salad relies on the quality of its ingredients, so make sure the spinach is young and fresh, and the mushrooms are firm and free from blemishes.

Preparation time:	**1 iceberg lettuce, sliced**
15–20 minutes	**2 bunches of watercress, trimmed and chopped**
Serves: **6**	**1 apple, peeled, cubed and tossed in lemon juice**
	25 g (1 oz) walnuts, chopped
	1 tablespoon walnut oil
	2 tablespoons wine vinegar
	salt and pepper

Mix the lettuce with the watercress and apple.

Sprinkle the walnuts over and drizzle on the walnut oil and vinegar. Season to taste. Toss the salad well just before serving.

Preparation time:	**4 unpeeled dessert apples, cored and diced**
15–20 minutes	**1 celery head, diced (reserve some leaves for garnish)**
Serves: **4–6**	**1 small bunch of grapes, halved and deseeded (optional)**
	50 g (2 oz) walnuts or pecan nuts, coarsely chopped
	mayonnaise

Mix the apples, celery, grapes and walnuts or pecan nuts with the mayonnaise, reserving some of the nuts to garnish.

Spoon into a bowl, arrange a few celery leaves around the edge and top with the remaining nuts.

COOK'S NOTES The partnership of apples with walnuts is ideal, but other fruit and nut combinations can work well. In summer try peaches and hazelnuts with hazelnut oil, for example, or apricots and almonds.

Preparation time:	**5 chicory heads, thinly sliced into rings**
15 minutes, plus	**(reserve several whole leaves for**
chilling	**garnish)**
	2 celery hearts, sliced thinly into rings
Serves: **4–6**	**4 oranges, peeled and segmented**
	250 g (8 oz) seedless white grapes
	250 g (8 oz) seedless black grapes
	2 bunches of watercress

CITRUS DRESSING:
9 tablespoons olive oil
3 tablespoons orange juice
1 tablespoon lemon juice
1 teaspoon caster sugar
2 spring onions, finely sliced
1 teaspoon freshly grated root ginger
salt and pepper

Toss together the chicory, celery, oranges and grapes. Separate the watercress into sprigs and set aside.

Make the dressing by mixing together all the ingredients and season to taste.

About 1 hour before serving, pour the dressing on to the salad. Toss to mix well and chill until required.

Add the watercress just before serving, and garnish with the reserved whole chicory leaves.

Preparation time:	**1 small ripe melon**
15 minutes	**125 g (4 oz) strawberries, hulled**
	8 cm (3 inch) piece of cucumber
Serves:	**1 small, crisp lettuce, shredded**
4 as a side salad or	**15 g (½ oz) flaked almonds, to garnish**
starter	

DRESSING:
4 tablespoons mayonnaise
2 tablespoons chopped lemon balm
salt and pepper

Cut the melon into quarters, then remove the seeds and skin. Cut the flesh into cubes, about 1 cm (½ inch) square, or scoop out balls.

Cut the strawberries and cucumber into thin slices.

To serve, arrange the shredded lettuce on a large serving dish or four individual plates. Arrange the pieces of melon, strawberry and cucumber on top of the lettuce.

To make the dressing, mix the mayonnaise with the chopped lemon balm and season to taste. Pour the dressing over the salad just before serving, and sprinkle with the almonds.

COOK'S NOTES Chicory has a crisp texture and bitter flavour which complements the sweetness of the fruit. Use radicchio instead if you can't get chicory.

COOK'S NOTES This salad is delicious served as a side dish with a selection of hard and soft cheeses and cold meats, such as ham, salami, air-dried beef and continental sausage.

71 Caesar salad

72 Warm salad niçoise

Preparation time:	**1 Cos lettuce**
15 minutes	**50 g (2 oz) can anchovy fillets in olive oil, drained**
Cooking time:	**75 g (3 oz) butter, melted**
12 minutes	**3 slices of day-old white bread, cubed**
	2 tablespoons freshly grated Parmesan
Oven temperature:	**salt and pepper**
200°C (400°F)	
Gas Mark 6	CAESAR DRESSING:
	5 tablespoons mayonnaise
Serves:	**4–5 tablespoons water**
4–6 as a side salad or	**1–2 garlic cloves**
starter	**1 tablespoon freshly grated Parmesan**

First make the dressing. Put the mayonnaise in a small bowl and stir in enough water to make a thin, pourable sauce. Crush the garlic to a paste with a little salt. Add to the mayonnaise with the Parmesan and stir well.

Tear the lettuce leaves into large pieces and place them in a large, shallow salad bowl. Snip the anchovies into small pieces and scatter them over the lettuce.

Toss the melted butter and bread together in a bowl until the bread is evenly coated, then spread the cubes out on a baking sheet. Place in a preheated oven, 200°C (400°F), Gas Mark 6, for about 10 minutes until golden and crisp.

To serve, tip the hot croûtons on to the salad and quickly drizzle the dressing over the top. Sprinkle over the Parmesan and serve at once.

Preparation time:	**about 250 g (8 oz) small new potatoes, scrubbed, or medium potatoes, scrubbed and quartered**
15 minutes	
Cooking time:	**5 tablespoons virgin olive oil**
30 minutes	**2 tablespoons red wine vinegar**
	250 g (8 oz) French beans
Serves: **2**	**250 g (8 oz) fresh tuna steak, cut into finger strips**
	2 garlic cloves, finely chopped
	2 anchovy fillets, chopped
	about 1½ teaspoons Dijon mustard
	1 red pepper, charred, skinned, cored, deseeded and thinly sliced
	2 tablespoons capers
	salt and pepper
	lemon wedges, to garnish (optional)

Steam the potatoes in a colander set over a saucepan of boiling water for 15–20 minutes or until just tender. Transfer to a serving bowl and toss gently with 1 tablespoon each of the olive oil and red wine vinegar. Season to taste.

Steam the French beans in the same way for 5–6 minutes until just tender. Set aside.

Heat another tablespoon of the oil in a nonstick frying pan, add the strips of tuna and sear evenly over a high heat. Add to the potato mixture.

Add the remaining olive oil to the frying pan and stir in the garlic and anchovies for 30 seconds. Stir in the remaining vinegar and boil for about 1 minute. Stir in the mustard then pour over the potato mixture.

Add the pepper strips, steamed beans, capers and more black pepper to the salad. Toss gently, taste and adjust the seasoning, if necessary. Serve immediately, garnished with lemon wedges, if liked.

4 Pizza, Noodles, Pasta and Rice

Preparation time:	**150 g (5 oz) strong wholemeal flour**
15 minutes, plus	**75 g (3 oz) unbleached strong plain flour**
rising	**1 teaspoon easy-blend dried yeast**
	1 teaspoon salt
Cooking time:	**1 tablespoon olive oil**
15–20 minutes	**125–150 ml (4–5 fl oz) warm water**
Makes:	
one 30 cm (12 inch)	
pizza or two 20 cm	
(8 inch) pizzas	

Sift together the flours, yeast and salt, and add the bran from the wholemeal flour to the bowl. Make a well in the centre and pour in the oil and water. Stir vigorously, gradually drawing in the flour to form a soft dough. Knead for at least 10 minutes until the dough feels smooth, elastic and springy.

Place the dough in an oiled bowl, turning once to coat it, then cover the bowl with a cloth and leave the dough to rise in a warm place for about 1½ hours or until it has doubled in size.

Use the dough as the base for your favourite pizza toppings or in one of the next three recipes instead of the base described.

COOK'S NOTES **To make basic white pizza dough, use 250 g (8 oz) strong plain flour, or Italian 00 flour, instead of the mixture of wholemeal and plain flours given in the recipe.**

Preparation time:	**3 tablespoons olive oil**
18–20 minutes	**2 red onions, finely sliced**
	2 garlic cloves, finely chopped
Cooking time:	**2 x 400 g (13 oz) cans chopped tomatoes**
10 minutes	**1 teaspoon red wine vinegar**
	sugar, to taste
Oven temperature:	**8 anchovy fillets, cut into thin lengths**
230°C (450°F)	**2 tablespoons pitted black olives**
Gas Mark 8	**1 tablespoon capers**
	250 g (8 oz) mozzarella, sliced
Serves: **4**	**salt and pepper**

BASIC PIZZA DOUGH:
250 g (8 oz) self-raising flour
1 teaspoon salt
150 ml (¼ pint) warm water

First make the base. Sift the flour and salt into a large bowl, then gradually add the water, mixing well to form a soft dough. When it has bound together, work the dough into a ball with your hands. Turn it out on a lightly floured surface and knead until it is smooth and soft.

Divide the dough into four and, with your hands and a rolling pin, flatten it as thinly as possible. The pizza rounds do not have to be exact circles, but make them slightly smaller than your serving plates.

Next make the topping. Heat the oil in a large saucepan. Add the onion and garlic and fry over a medium heat, stirring frequently, for 3 minutes. Add the tomatoes, vinegar and sugar and season to taste. Increase the heat and simmer, stirring from time to time, until the mixture has reduced by half to make a thick, rich tomato sauce.

Place the pizza bases on warmed baking sheets, spoon over the sauce and spread to the edge with the back of a spoon.

Arrange the anchovies on the pizzas, sprinkle with the olives and capers and finally add the moz)zarella. Bake the pizzas in a preheated oven, 230°C (450°F), Gas Mark 8, for 10 minutes until they are golden and sizzling.

75 Artichoke and mushroom pizza

76 Roasted vegetable pizza

Preparation time:
10 minutes

Cooking time:
15 minutes

Oven temperature:
240°C (475°F)
Gas Mark 9

Makes:
one 30 cm (12 inch)
pizza

Basic Pizza Dough (see recipe 74)
400 g (13 oz) can artichokes in oil,
drained (reserve the oil)
1 tablespoon lemon juice, or to taste
2 tablespoons olive oil
125 g (4 oz) oyster mushrooms, sliced
125 g (4 oz) mozzarella, grated
1 tablespoon chopped oregano

Roll out the dough to a 30 cm (12 inch) circle, making the edge slightly thicker than the centre, and place it on an oiled, perforated pizza pan.

Pour the oil from the artichokes into a bowl, stir in lemon juice to taste and use the mixture to brush over the pizza base. Slice the artichokes in half.

Heat the olive oil in a frying pan, add the oyster mushrooms and fry for 5–6 minutes. Toss the mushrooms with the artichokes and spread evenly over the pizza base. Scatter over the grated mozzarella.

Bake in a preheated oven, 240°C (475°F), Gas Mark 9, for about 15 minutes. Garnish with the chopped oregano and serve immediately.

COOK'S NOTES This pizza is made with a simple scone base to save time. For the real thing, follow recipe 73 which uses yeast in the dough.

Preparation time:
20 minutes, plus
rising

Cooking time:
55 minutes

Oven temperature:
200°C (400°F)
Gas Mark 6

Makes:
one 30 cm (12 inch)
pizza

SUN-DRIED TOMATO DOUGH:
250 g (8 oz) unbleached strong plain flour
1 teaspoon easy-blend dried yeast
1 teaspoon salt
25 g (1 oz) sun-dried tomatoes, chopped
1 tablespoon olive oil
125–150 ml (4–5 fl oz) warm water

TOPPING:
1 aubergine, sliced
1 yellow pepper, deseeded and sliced
1 red onion, cut into small wedges
1 courgette, cut into sticks
3 garlic cloves, thickly sliced
3 tablespoons olive oil
2 teaspoons chopped rosemary
2–3 tablespoons tomato paste
2 tablespoons grated Parmesan
salt and pepper

To make the dough, sift the dry ingredients into a bowl. Make a well in the centre and add the tomatoes and oil. Gradually pour in the water, stirring to draw in the flour a little at a time to form a soft dough. Knead the dough for 10 minutes until it feels smooth and springy. Place the dough in an oiled bowl, cover with a cloth and leave to rise in a warm place for 1–2 hours until the dough has doubled in size. When the dough has risen sufficiently, knock it back and turn it out on to a floured surface. Knead it again for 2–3 minutes, then roll out to a 30 cm (12 inch) circle and place it on a greased baking sheet.

Mix all the vegetables in a roasting tin with the garlic, oil and rosemary and season to taste. Place the roasting tin in a preheated oven, 200°C (400°F), Gas Mark 6, and roast for 35 minutes or until the vegetables are tender. Spread the tomato paste over the dough. Arrange the roasted vegetables on the top and sprinkle over the Parmesan. Season to taste. Bake the pizza in the oven for 20 minutes. Serve immediately.

Preparation time: **25 minutes, plus rising**

Cooking time: **35 minutes**

Oven temperature: **200°C (400°F) Gas Mark 6, then 190°C (375°F) Gas Mark 5**

Makes: **one 30 cm (12 inch) calzone**

DOUGH:
25 g (1 oz) fresh yeast
4–5 tablespoons warm milk
325 g (11 oz) strong plain flour
½ teaspoon salt
25 g (1 oz) sugar
150 g (5 oz) butter, cubed
2 eggs, beaten

FILLING:
175 g (6 oz) mozzarella, sliced
50 g (2 oz) pecorino, grated
150 g (5 oz) smoked raw or cooked ham, cut into thin strips
2 tomatoes, skinned, deseeded and sliced
beaten egg, to glaze
salt and pepper

To make the dough, dissolve the yeast in the milk. Sift the flour and salt on to a large board or work surface. Stir in the sugar and make a well in the centre. Add the butter, eggs and the dissolved yeast and work the ingredients together to make a smooth dough. Knead well until the dough is pliable, then shape it into a ball. Put the dough in a bowl sprinkled with flour, cover it with a cloth and leave to rise at room temperature for 2 hours or until the dough has doubled in size. Knead the dough for 5 minutes, then roll it out to a 30 cm (12 inch) circle.

Put half the mozzarella and half the pecorino on one half of the circle, add a layer of ham, then make another layer with the remaining cheeses and top with the tomato slices, seasoning the layers as you go. Brush the edge of the dough with water, fold over and press the edges together to seal, then brush the top with beaten egg.

Bake the calzone in a preheated oven, 200°C (400°F), Gas Mark 6, for 15 minutes, then lower the temperature to 190°C (375°F), Gas Mark 5, and bake for a further 20 minutes. Serve immediately.

Preparation time: **35 minutes**

Cooking time: **30–40 minutes**

Serves: **4 as a first course or 3–4 as a light main dish**

750 g (1½ lb) floury old potatoes
125 g (4 oz) plain flour, sifted
25 g (1 oz) butter, diced
1 egg yolk, beaten
salt and pepper
pesto, to serve

TO GARNISH:
15 g (½ oz) butter (optional)
50 g (2 oz) freshly grated Parmesan

Boil the potatoes in their skins and drain them thoroughly. When they are cool enough to handle, peel them and push through a coarse sieve or medium food mill into the same pan. Allow them to dry out by stirring for a few moments over gentle heat, then turn them into a bowl and beat in the sifted flour, butter and egg yolk. Season to taste. Turn out the dough on to a floured board and knead lightly once or twice, then cut it in 4 pieces. Form each piece into a roll about 2.5 cm (1 inch) thick. Leave the dough to rest for about 10 minutes.

Bring a large pan of lightly salted water to the boil. Cut the rolls of potato dough into slices about 1 cm (½ inch) thick, and press each one gently in the palm of your hand, using a fork to give a ridged effect.

When all are done, drop them, a few at a time, into the gently simmering water. Cook for about 3 minutes after the water comes back to the boil. Shortly after the gnocchi rise to the surface, lift them out with a slotted spoon and drain while you cook the next batch. Transfer the drained gnocchi to a heated serving dish. When all are cooked, add just enough pesto to give a generous coating folding it in lightly, then dot with butter, if using, and sprinkle with a little freshly grated Parmesan. Serve immediately, with the remaining Parmesan in a small bowl.

COOK'S NOTES Classic pesto is now widely available. Some larger supermarkets and specialist delis also have rocket pesto, which makes a delicious alternative. Another way to serve gnocchi is to drizzle it with butter and sprinkle torn sage leaves over the cooked shapes.

Preparation time:	250 g (8 oz) Chinese rice noodles
10 minutes	2 tablespoons vegetable oil
	3–4 spring onions, thinly sliced
Cooking time:	2.5 cm (1 inch) fresh root ginger, chopped
10 minutes	1 garlic clove, crushed
	2 skinless chicken breasts, each about
Serves: 4	150 g (5 oz), cut into thin strips
	125 g (4 oz) mangetout
	125 g (4 oz) lean cooked ham, shredded
	75 g (3 oz) bean sprouts
	pepper

SAUCE:
2 teaspoons cornflour
8 tablespoons Chicken Stock (see
    introduction) or water
2 tablespoons soy sauce
2 tablespoons sake or dry sherry
2 teaspoons sesame oil

Cook the rice noodles according to the packet instructions.

To make the sauce, mix the cornflour with 2 tablespoons of the stock or water to make a smooth paste. Stir in the remaining stock or water and the soy sauce, sake or sherry and the sesame oil. Set aside.

Drain the noodles, rinse them under cold water and set aside.

Preheat a wok or large frying pan. Add the oil, swirl it around and heat over a moderate heat until hot. Add the spring onions, ginger and garlic and stir-fry for 1–2 minutes or until softened but not browned. Add the chicken, increase the heat to high and stir-fry for 3–4 minutes or until lightly coloured on all sides.

Add the mangetout and stir-fry for 1–2 minutes or until just tender, then add the ham and bean sprouts and stir-fry to mix. Stir the sauce, pour it into the pan and bring to the boil, stirring constantly. Add the drained noodles and toss until combined and piping hot. Season with pepper to taste and serve immediately.

Preparation time:	500 g (1 lb) thin asparagus spears,
10 minutes	trimmed
	3–4 tablespoons olive oil
Cooking time:	juice of 1 lemon
20–25 minutes	375 g (12 oz) spaghetti
	2 garlic cloves, roughly chopped
Serves: 4	¼–½ teaspoon dried chilli flakes
	25 g (1 oz) basil leaves
	25 g (1 oz) freshly grated Parmesan, plus
	extra to serve
	salt and pepper

Brush the asparagus spears with a little oil and griddle or grill them until they are charred and tender. Toss with a little more oil and half of the lemon juice, season to taste and set aside.

Bring a large saucepan of lightly salted water to the boil and plunge in the spaghetti. Bring the water back to the boil and simmer according to the instructions on the packet or for 10–12 minutes until it is tender but firm to the bite (al dente).

Just before the pasta is cooked, heat the remaining oil in a large frying pan or wok and cook the garlic with a little salt for 3–4 minutes until it is softened but not browned. Add the chilli flakes and asparagus and heat through.

Drain the pasta, reserving 4 tablespoons of the cooking liquid, and add both to the pan with the basil, the remaining lemon juice, pepper and Parmesan. Serve immediately with extra Parmesan, if liked.

COOK'S NOTES Cook pasta in the largest saucepan you have. It will not stick together if it is cooked in plenty of water. Adding a dash of oil will help prevent the boiling water from frothing. Make sure the water is boiling before you add the pasta.

81 Spaghetti with rocket and ricotta

82 Spaghetti with courgette and carrot ribbons

Preparation time:
10 minutes

Cooking time:
12 minutes

Serves: 4

300 g (10 oz) spaghetti
2 teaspoons olive oil
1 small onion, finely chopped
1 bunch of rocket, roots trimmed and
**   leaves finely chopped**
1 garlic clove, finely chopped
75 g (3 oz) ricotta
125 ml (4 fl oz) dry white wine
salt and pepper

Bring a large saucepan of lightly salted water to the boil and plunge in the spaghetti. Bring the water back to the boil and simmer according to the instructions on the packet or for 10–12 minutes until it is tender but firm to the bite (al dente).

Meanwhile, heat the oil in a frying pan and add the onion. Cook gently, stirring for 5–10 minutes or until softened.

Add the rocket and garlic and season to taste. Cook, stirring, for 2–3 minutes until the rocket is wilted. Add the ricotta and wine and stir until the ricotta has melted and is mixed evenly with the rocket.

Drain the spaghetti, return to the pan and add the rocket mixture. Toss well to combine and serve immediately.

Preparation time:
10 minutes

Cooking time:
25–30 minutes

Serves: 4

300 g (10 oz) spaghetti
3 carrots
3 courgettes
15 g (½ oz) butter
1 tablespoon olive oil
2 garlic cloves, crushed
75 g (3 oz) finely chopped basil
40 g (1½ oz) finely chopped parsley
25 g (1 oz) snipped chives
2 tablespoons finely chopped marjoram
½ small radicchio, shredded
salt and pepper
Parmesan shavings, to garnish

Bring a large saucepan of lightly salted water to the boil and plunge in the spaghetti. Bring the water back to the boil and simmer according to the instructions on the packet or for 10–12 minutes until it is tender but firm to the bite (al dente).

Meanwhile, slice the carrots and courgettes into long, thin strips, to resemble spaghetti.

Melt the butter with the oil in a large frying pan. Add the garlic and carrots and cook, stirring, for 5–7 minutes.

Drain the spaghetti and add to the frying pan with the courgette strips, basil, parsley, chives and marjoram. Stir to mix, season to taste and cook for 4–5 minutes until the courgettes are cooked through.

Remove the pan from the heat and transfer the spaghetti and vegetable mixture to a warmed serving dish. Add the shredded radicchio and toss to mix. Sprinkle with the Parmesan shavings and serve immediately.

COOK'S NOTES Rocket, also known as arugula, is a **Mediterranean plant with a pungent, slightly peppery taste. The young leaves are particularly good in salads and pasta dishes. If you like, use spinach instead of rocket, but be generous with the pepper.**

Preparation time: **10 minutes**	**1 kg (2 lb) fresh clams, scrubbed** **7 tablespoons water** **7 tablespoons olive oil**
Cooking time: **30 minutes**	**1 garlic clove, sliced** **425 g (14 oz) tomatoes, skinned and finely chopped**
Serves: **4**	**425 g (14 oz) spaghetti** **1 tablespoon chopped parsley** **salt and pepper**

Put the clams in a large saucepan with the water and cook until the shells open. Remove the clams from the shells. Strain the cooking liquid and reserve for later.

Heat the oil in a large frying pan, add the garlic and cook gently for 5 minutes. Remove and discard the garlic, then add the tomatoes and the reserved cooking liquid to the pan. Stir and simmer for 20 minutes.

Meanwhile, bring a large saucepan of lightly salted water to the boil and plunge in the spaghetti. Bring the water back to the boil and simmer according to the instructions on the packet or for 10–12 minutes until it is tender but firm to the bite (al dente). Drain thoroughly.

Add the clams and parsley to the tomato sauce and heat thoroughly for 1 minute. Pile the spaghetti in a warmed serving dish, add the sauce, season to taste and fork gently to mix. Serve immediately.

Preparation time: **10 minutes**	**4 tablespoons olive oil** **2 onions, chopped** **2 garlic cloves, finely chopped**
Cooking time: **about 30 minutes**	**8 anchovy fillets, coarsely chopped** **400 g (13 oz) can plum tomatoes, drained and roughly chopped**
Serves: **4**	**12 black olives, pitted and halved** **1 tablespoon capers, drained** **2 tablespoons chopped oregano** **300 g (10 oz) fusilli or other dried pasta shapes** **125 g (4 oz) freshly grated Parmesan** **salt and pepper** **red basil leaves, to garnish**

Heat the oil in a saucepan over a moderate heat, add the onions and cook gently for 5–10 minutes until softened. Add the garlic and anchovies and cook for a further 3 minutes or until the anchovies disintegrate into the sauce.

Stir in the tomatoes, olives, capers and oregano, and season to taste. Simmer the sauce gently for about 20 minutes, stirring occasionally.

Meanwhile, bring a large saucepan of lightly salted water to the boil and plunge in the pasta. Bring the water back to the boil and simmer according to the instructions on the packet or for 8–10 minutes until it is tender but firm to the bite (al dente).

Drain the pasta thoroughly, then toss it with the sauce. Serve immediately, sprinkled with the Parmesan and garnished with red basil leaves.

COOK'S NOTES Fresh clams in their shells should be well scrubbed before they are cooked. Discard any shells which are open, unless they shut tightly when tapped.

COOK'S NOTES If you prefer to use fresh pasta instead of dry, remember that the cooking time will be no more than 3–4 minutes – less for small shapes.

Preparation time: **15 minutes**	**6 unsmoked streaky bacon rashers**
	2 tablespoons olive oil
	2 fennel bulbs, finely chopped
Cooking time: **15–20 minutes**	**2 garlic cloves, finely chopped**
	4 tablespoons freshly grated Parmesan
	300 ml (½ pint) fromage frais
Serves: **4–6**	**3 tablespoons finely chopped parsley**
	375 g (12 oz) green tagliatelle
	salt and pepper
	fennel fronds, to garnish

Grill the bacon until it is crisp. Drain on kitchen paper and set aside. Heat the oil in a pan and add the fennel and garlic. Cover the pan and cook gently over a low heat for 5 minutes or until the fennel is tender.

Add the Parmesan, fromage frais and parsley to the pan and season to taste. Simmer over a low heat for 1–2 minutes.

Meanwhile, bring a large saucepan of lightly salted water to the boil and plunge in the pasta. Bring the water back to the boil and simmer according to the instructions on the packet or for 8–10 minutes until it is tender but firm to the bite (al dente). Drain and toss with the sauce. Transfer to a warmed serving dish.

Chop the bacon and sprinkle over the pasta. Garnish with fennel fronds and serve immediately.

Preparation time: **10 minutes**	**4 tablespoons olive oil**
	2 onions, chopped
	2 garlic cloves, crushed
Cooking time: **about 20 minutes**	**500 g (1 lb) plum tomatoes, skinned and chopped**
	2 tablespoons tomato purée
Serves: **4**	**1 teaspoon sugar**
	100 ml (3½ fl oz) dry white wine
	handful of ripe olives, pitted and quartered
	handful of torn basil leaves
	375 g (12 oz) dried tagliatelle
	salt and pepper
	50 g (2 oz) Parmesan shavings, to serve

Heat 3 tablespoons of the olive oil in a large frying pan. Add the onion and garlic and cook gently over low heat until they are soft and slightly coloured. Stir the mixture occasionally.

Add the tomatoes, tomato purée, sugar and wine, stirring well. Continue to cook over gentle heat until the mixture is quite thick and reduced. Stir in the quartered olives and torn basil leaves, and season to taste.

Meanwhile, bring a large saucepan of lightly salted water to the boil and plunge in the pasta. Bring the water back to the boil and simmer according to the instructions on the packet or for 8–10 minutes until it is tender but firm to the bite (al dente).

Drain the tagliatelle thoroughly and immediately mix in the remaining olive oil and a generous grinding of black pepper. Arrange the pasta on four serving plates and top with the tomato sauce, mixing it into the tagliatelle. Serve with large curls of shaved Parmesan.

COOK'S NOTES Green tagliatelle (tagliatelle verde) is made with spinach, which gives the colour. Spinach is used to make a wide range of green pasta, which is a good contrast to the sauces in many pasta dishes.

Preparation time: **10 minutes**

Cooking time: **30 minutes**

Serves: **4**

3 tablespoons olive oil
75 g (3 oz) rindless smoked bacon, cubed
1 onion, finely chopped
5 sage leaves, plus extra to garnish (optional)
250 g (8 oz) can borlotti beans
2 tablespoons Chicken Stock (see introduction)
¼ teaspoon flour
1 tablespoon tomato purée
2 tablespoons red wine
425 g (14 oz) dried tagliatelle
2 tablespoons grated Parmesan
1 tablespoon grated pecorino

Heat the oil in a large pan, add the bacon, onion and whole sage leaves. Cook over a medium heat until golden.

Drain the beans, rinse and drain again, then add them to the pan.

Heat the stock. Mix the flour and tomato purée in a small bowl, stir in the hot stock and the wine. Pour the sauce into the bean mixture, stir with a wooden spoon and simmer over a low heat until the sauce starts to thicken.

Meanwhile, bring a large saucepan of lightly salted water to the boil and plunge in the pasta. Bring the water back to the boil and simmer according to the instructions on the packet or for 8–10 minutes until it is tender but firm to the bite (al dente).

Remove the sage leaves from the sauce, taste and adjust the seasoning. Drain the pasta thoroughly and mix it with the sauce. Put the pasta in a large, warmed serving dish. Add the Parmesan and pecorino and serve hot, garnished with a few fresh sage leaves.

Preparation time: **15–20 minutes**

Cooking time: **50 minutes–1 hour**

Serves: **4**

1–2 tablespoons olive oil
1 large onion, finely chopped
2 garlic cloves, crushed
125 g (4 oz) rindless streaky bacon, chopped
1–2 fresh red chillies, chopped
425 g (14 oz) can chopped tomatoes
50–75 g (2–3 oz) pecorino or Parmesan, shaved
500 g (1 lb) penne
salt and pepper

Heat the oil in a pan and cook the onion, garlic and bacon until they are lightly coloured.

Add the chillies, tomatoes and 25 g (1 oz) of the cheese. Season to taste. Cook over a gentle heat for 30–40 minutes until the sauce thickens. Check the seasoning again.

Meanwhile, bring a large saucepan of lightly salted water to the boil and plunge in the pasta. Bring the water back to the boil and simmer according to the instructions on the packet or for 10–12 minutes until it is tender but firm to the bite (al dente). Drain well and place in a hot serving dish.

Stir most of the sauce into the pasta, mix well and pour the remaining sauce over the top. Garnish with curls of pecorino or Parmesan and serve the remaining cheese separately.

COOK'S NOTES You can buy red or green chillies – the red ones are hotter. For a milder taste slice the chillies in half lengthways and scrape out the seeds before chopping them. Take care that you do not touch your eyes or mouth while you are handling chillies.

89 Penne with spicy sausage sauce

90 Baked pasta with pepper sauce

Preparation time:	**3 tablespoons oil**
10 minutes	**25 g (1 oz) butter**
	½ onion, chopped
Cooking time:	**1 shallot, chopped**
15 minutes	**1 small carrot, finely sliced**
	1 celery stick, sliced
Serves: **4**	**125 g (4 oz) salamelle sausage, crumbled**
	½ small yellow pepper, deseeded and diced
	4 basil leaves, torn
	50 ml (2 fl oz) dry red wine
	425 g (14 oz) penne
	2 tablespoons grated pecorino
	2 tablespoons grated Parmesan
	whole basil leaves, to garnish

Heat the oil and butter in a flameproof casserole, add the onion, shallot, carrot and celery and cook over low heat for 4 minutes. Mix well. Add the crumbled sausages, diced pepper and torn basil to the casserole. Brown over medium heat for 3–4 minutes and moisten with red wine.

Meanwhile, bring a large saucepan of lightly salted water to the boil and plunge in the pasta. Bring the water back to the boil and simmer according to the instructions on the packet or for 10–12 minutes until it is tender but firm to the bite (al dente).

Drain the pasta and transfer it to a warmed serving dish. Pour over the sausage and vegetable sauce.

Sprinkle with the cheeses and mix well before serving, garnished with whole basil leaves.

COOK'S NOTES Look around specialist Italian food stores or the delicatessen counters of supermarkets to find the spicy salamelle cooking sausage. If you can't get this, use continental sausage or any good quality sausage.

Preparation time:	**2 large yellow peppers, cored, deseeded and finely chopped**
20 minutes	**½ onion, finely chopped**
Cooking time:	**6 plum tomatoes, skinned and chopped**
35–40 minutes	**250 ml (8 fl oz) Vegetable Stock (see introduction)**
Oven temperature:	**375 g (12 oz) penne or other pasta shapes**
200°C (400°F)	**½ teaspoon chopped basil**
Gas Mark 6	**200 g (7 oz) mozzarella, diced**
	3 tablespoons milk
Serves: **4**	**salt and pepper**
	shredded basil leaves, to garnish

Place the peppers in a saucepan with the onion, tomatoes and a pinch of salt. Cover the pan and cook for 5 minutes. Add the stock and continue to simmer for a further 15 minutes.

Meanwhile, bring a large saucepan of lightly salted water to the boil and plunge in the pasta. Bring the water back to the boil and simmer according to the instructions on the packet or for 8–10 minutes until it is tender but firm to the bite (al dente). Drain thoroughly.

Sprinkle the basil over the pepper sauce and season to taste. Mix the sauce with the drained pasta and the diced mozzarella. Transfer to a large, greased ovenproof dish, pour over the milk and place in a preheated oven, 200°C (400°F), Gas Mark 6, for about 15 minutes or until golden-brown. Serve immediately, garnished with shredded basil.

91 Macaroni with anchovies

Preparation time: **10 minutes**

Cooking time: **30 minutes**

Serves: **4**

2 anchovy fillets
4 tablespoons oil
1 garlic clove, peeled
50 g (2 oz) smoked bacon, diced
425 g (14 oz) can plum tomatoes
50 g (2 oz) pitted black olives, chopped
¼ teaspoon chopped oregano
375 g (12 oz) macaroni
25 g (1 oz) pecorino, grated
salt and pepper

Heat the oil in a small pan and add the whole garlic clove and drained anchovies. Cook over medium heat for a few minutes, then remove the garlic and add the bacon.

Drain the tomatoes and cut them into strips. When the bacon is crisp, add the tomatoes to the pan. Season to taste and leave to cook over low heat, stirring from time to time, for about 20 minutes or until the mixture has reduced to a thick sauce. Add the olives and oregano halfway through the cooking time.

Meanwhile, bring a large saucepan of lightly salted water to the boil and plunge in the pasta. Bring the water back to the boil and simmer according to the instructions on the packet or for 10–12 minutes until it is tender but firm to the bite (al dente).

Drain the pasta thoroughly and transfer it to a warmed serving dish. Pour over the sauce and sprinkle with the grated pecorino. Mix well before serving.

COOK'S NOTES Anchovy fillets can be rather salty. If you like, soak them in a little milk for 10 minutes before use to remove some of the salt.

92 Mussel risotto

Preparation time: **30 minutes**

Cooking time: **20 minutes**

Serves: **4**

1 kg (2 lb) mussels in their shells
1 teaspoon oil
1 small onion, roughly chopped
1 garlic clove, roughly chopped
150 ml (¼ pint) Fish Stock (see introduction) or white wine

RISOTTO:
1 tablespoon olive oil
2 small onions, finely chopped
1–2 garlic cloves, finely chopped
375 g (12 oz) arborio rice
1 litre (1¾ pints) Fish Stock (see introduction)
Parmesan shavings, to serve (optional)
salt and pepper

Wash the mussels in plenty of cold water, discarding any that do not close when tapped sharply. Heat the oil in a large pan, add the onion and garlic and cook for several minutes. Add the fish stock or white wine and the mussels. Heat briskly until the mussels open. Strain and reserve the cooking liquid. Remove the mussel flesh from both their shells. Do not try to force open any shells which have not opened properly – simply discard them.

To make the risotto, heat the oil and cook the onions for 5 minutes, then add the garlic and continue to cook gently until the onion is soft. Add the rice and stir over a low heat until the rice is coated.

Meanwhile, heat the fish stock, and add the reserved liquid from cooking the mussels. Add the stock a ladleful at a time and cook steadily, stirring, until the rice has absorbed the liquid, then add more of the stock. Continue in this way until the rice is almost tender.

Gently stir in the shelled mussels, reserving a few in their shells to garnish, and enough of the hot stock needed to produce the correct texture. Season to taste and heat for the last few minutes. Serve immediately with Parmesan shavings, if liked.

Preparation time:	**125 g (4 oz) unsalted butter, softened**
5–10 minutes	**1 onion, finely chopped**
	3–4 tablespoons dry white wine
Cooking time:	**400 g (13 oz) arborio rice**
30–40 minutes	**1 litre (1¾ pints) hot Beef Stock (see introduction), kept simmering**
Serves: **4–6**	**125 g (4 oz) freshly grated Parmesan salt and pepper**
	Parmesan shavings, to garnish
	radicchio and rocket leaves, to serve

Preparation time:	**375 g (12 oz) courgettes, quartered**
10 minutes, plus	**lengthways and cut into chunks**
draining	**3 tablespoons olive oil**
	1 small onion, chopped
Cooking time:	**300 g (10 oz) arborio rice**
30–35 minutes	**1 litre (1¾ pints) hot Chicken Stock (see introduction), kept simmering**
Serves: **4**	**25 g (1 oz) butter**
	3 tablespoons freshly grated Parmesan
	salt and pepper

Melt half of the butter in a large frying pan, add the onion and cook gently for 5–10 minutes until softened. Season to taste. Add the wine and boil until it evaporates.

Add the rice and cook, stirring, for 1–2 minutes until it has absorbed the onion and wine mixture. Add a ladleful of the hot stock and cook over medium-low heat, stirring, until it has been absorbed. Continue adding the stock, a ladleful at a time, stirring constantly and adding more stock as it is absorbed. When all the stock has been absorbed, which will take 20–25 minutes, remove the pan from the heat, add the remaining butter and the Parmesan and fold in gently.

Transfer to warmed plates, sprinkle with the Parmesan shavings and a generous grinding of black pepper, and serve immediately with radicchio and rocket leaves.

Put the courgettes into a colander and sprinkle with salt. Leave to drain for 30 minutes, then rinse and pat dry on kitchen paper.

Heat 2 tablespoons of the oil in a saucepan, add the courgettes and fry until they are slightly darkened. Remove them from the pan and set aside. Heat the remaining oil in the pan, add the onion and fry for 5 minutes, stirring occasionally.

Add the rice, stirring until all the grains are coated with oil. Add a ladleful of the stock and bring to the boil. Simmer, stirring, until all the liquid has been absorbed. Continue adding the stock in this way until all the liquid has been absorbed and the rice is creamy.

Stir in the courgettes, season to taste and heat through. Remove the pan from the heat, and quickly stir in the butter and cheese. Transfer to a warmed serving dish and serve immediately.

COOK'S NOTES Use the best quality Parmesan for this recipe and grate it just before you add it to the dish.

95 Rocket risotto

96 Mushroom risotto

Preparation time: **5 minutes**	**1 teaspoon olive oil** **1 onion, finely chopped** **300 g (10 oz) arborio rice**
Cooking time: **25–35 minutes**	**1.2 litres (2 pints) hot Vegetable Stock** **(see introduction), kept simmering** **50 g (2 oz) rocket leaves**
Serves: **4**	**salt and pepper**

Heat the oil in a large frying pan, add the onion and cook gently for 5–10 minutes until softened. Add the rice and stir well to coat the grains in the oil.

Set the pan over a medium heat and add just enough stock to cover the rice. Stir continuously until the stock is absorbed into the rice. Keep on adding the stock a little at a time, stirring until it is all absorbed. This will take about 20 minutes.

Stir in the rocket, reserving 4 leaves for garnish, and cook briefly, until the leaves start to wilt. Season to taste and serve immediately, each portion garnished with a rocket leaf.

Preparation time: **30 minutes**	**15 g (½ oz) butter or margarine** **1 onion, sliced** **250 g (8 oz) medium-grain brown rice**
Cooking time: **about 20 minutes**	**150 ml (¼ pint) dry white wine** **600 ml (1 pint) hot Vegetable Stock or** **Chicken Stock (see introduction), kept**
Serves: **4**	**simmering** **250 g (8 oz) mushrooms, sliced** **1 tablespoon chopped basil** **1 tablespoon grated Parmesan** **salt and pepper**

Melt the fat in a frying pan and cook the onion until it is golden. Stir in the rice, making sure that all the grains are coated, and cook for 5 minutes, stirring frequently.

Add the wine and bring to the boil until well reduced. Stir in a ladleful of the stock, the mushrooms, basil and seasoning to taste. Simmer, stirring, until all the liquid has been absorbed. Keep on adding the stock a little at a time, stirring until it is all absorbed. This will take 20 minutes or more.

Stir in the grated Parmesan and serve immediately.

COOK'S NOTES A risotto should have a soft, creamy texture, which is achieved by using the right kind of rice and adding the liquid gradually during the cooking process. To enjoy a risotto at its best, it should be served immediately after cooking.

Preparation time: **10 minutes, plus soaking**	**150 g (5 oz) fresh morels, rinsed, trimmed and halved lengthways, or 15 g (½ oz) dried morels, 5 g (¼ oz) dried horn of plenty and 125 g (4 oz) mixed fresh mushrooms (such as shiitake, yellow and grey oyster mushrooms), trimmed**
Cooking time: **about 30 minutes**	**150 g (5 oz) wild rice, well rinsed**
Serves: **2**	**50 g (2 oz) butter** **75 ml (3 fl oz) double cream** **1 tablespoon brandy** **salt and pepper**

If you are using dried mushrooms soak them in a bowl of warm water for 20–30 minutes. Drain thoroughly.

Place the wild rice in a large saucepan of lightly salted, boiling water and cook for 18–20 minutes until the grains begin to split. Drain well.

Meanwhile, melt half the butter in a frying pan, add all the mushrooms and cook over a moderately high heat for 2–3 minutes. Season to taste. Add the cream and brandy, stir to mix, then reduce the heat and continue cooking until the liquid has almost all evaporated. Transfer the mushrooms to a bowl, cover and keep warm.

Melt the remaining butter in the pan, add the wild rice and reheat, stirring to coat the grains with the buttery juices. Season to taste and serve immediately, topped with the mushrooms.

Preparation time: **5 minutes, plus soaking**	**250 g (8 oz) dried red kidney beans** **900 ml (1½ pints) boiling water** **600 ml (1 pint) coconut milk** **2 thyme sprigs**
Cooking time: **55 minutes**	**2 spring onions, finely chopped** **1 fresh green chilli, deseeded and finely chopped**
Serves: **6**	**500 g (1 lb) long-grain rice** **salt and pepper** **thyme sprigs, to garnish**

Put the dried red kidney beans into a large bowl and cover with cold water. Leave to soak overnight.

Rinse the kidney beans thoroughly and drain well. Put them into a large saucepan, add the boiling water and cook for about 30 minutes or until the kidney beans are almost tender.

Add the coconut milk, thyme, spring onions and chilli to the pan. Season to taste and bring back to the boil. Boil rapidly for 5 minutes.

Add the rice and stir well. Cover and reduce the heat, so that the mixture simmers gently until all the liquid has been absorbed. This will take 20–25 minutes. If there is any liquid left in the pan, drain the rice and beans and transfer them to a warmed dish. Garnish with fresh thyme sprigs and serve hot.

COOK'S NOTES For a quicker version, use canned red kidney beans instead of dried. This will avoid the need for soaking and cooking in boiling water. Simply put them in a saucepan with 600 ml (1 pint) of boiling water and continue with the recipe from paragraph 3.

Preparation time:	250 g (8 oz) long-grain rice
15 minutes	1 onion, chopped
	1–2 tablespoons Chicken Stock or
	Vegetable Stock (see introduction)
Cooking time:	1 teaspoon ground turmeric
20 minutes	1 tablespoon currants
	250 g (8 oz) can pineapple pieces,
Serves: **4**	drained
	salt

Cook the rice in lightly salted boiling water for 10 minutes or according to the instructions on the packet. Drain and sprinkle with a little cold water to separate the grains. Keep the rice warm in a covered dish.

Cook the onion until tender in a little stock and add the turmeric, currants and pineapple pieces to warm through. Drain. Toss the rice in this mixture and serve immediately.

Preparation time:	500 g (1 lb) smoked haddock, soaked in
25 minutes	cold water
	1 small onion, finely chopped
Cooking time:	2 tablespoons Fish Stock or Vegetable
about 20 minutes	Stock (see introduction)
	1 teaspoon curry powder
Serves: **4**	250 g (8 oz) long-grain rice
	1 bay leaf
	juice of 1 lemon
	3 tablespoons chopped parsley
	pepper
	lemon wedges, to serve

Bring a large pan of fresh water to the boil, add the drained haddock and simmer for a few minutes until it is tender. Drain and flake the fish.

Cook the onion in the stock until it is soft, then sprinkle over the curry powder and cook for 1 minute longer.

Meanwhile, cook the rice and bay leaf in plenty of lightly salted boiling water for 10 minutes. Remove and discard the bay leaf, drain the rice and sprinkle over a few drops of cold water to separate the grains and stop the rice from cooking further.

Combine the flaked haddock, the onion mixture and the rice. Grind plenty of black pepper into the kedgeree and sprinkle over the lemon juice and parsley. Toss lightly and pile into a hot dish.

Serve with lemon wedges.

COOK'S NOTES Turmeric comes from the same family as ginger, and it can be used fresh, like ginger. It has bright orange flesh, which turns yellow when dried. It is also available dried, either whole or ground, but is probably best bought ground because it is so hard.

5 Vegetarian Dishes

101 Mushroom and chickpea curry

Preparation time:
10 minutes

Cooking time:
25 minutes

Serves: **4**

50 g (2 oz) butter
1 onion, chopped
2 garlic cloves, crushed
2.5 cm (1 inch) fresh root ginger, peeled and grated
250 g (8 oz) button mushrooms
2 tablespoons hot curry powder
1 teaspoon ground coriander
1 teaspoon ground cinnamon
½ teaspoon turmeric
375 g (12 oz) potatoes, diced
425 g (14 oz) can chickpeas, drained and rinsed
50 g (2 oz) cashew nuts, toasted and chopped (optional)
125 ml (4 fl oz) Greek yogurt
2 tablespoons chopped fresh coriander
salt and pepper

Melt the butter in a larger frying pan and cook the onion, garlic, ginger and mushrooms for 5 minutes.

Add the curry powder, coriander, cinnamon, turmeric and potatoes and mix together. Add the chickpeas and season to taste. Add just enough water to cover the ingredients, bring to the boil, cover and simmer gently for 15 minutes.

If you are using them, stir the cashew nuts into the curry together with the yogurt and chopped fresh coriander. Heat through gently and serve with rice.

COOK'S NOTES Do not let the curry boil after you have added the yogurt or it may curdle. Simply heat the mixture through gently until hot.

102 Soya beans with spinach

Preparation time:
15 minutes, plus soaking

Cooking time:
1½ hours

Serves: **4**

175 g (6 oz) soya beans, soaked overnight, drained and rinsed
3 tablespoons olive oil
1 garlic clove, chopped
1 teaspoon grated fresh root ginger
2 red chillies, deseeded and chopped
125 g (4 oz) shiitake mushrooms, sliced
4 ripe tomatoes, skinned, deseeded and chopped
2 tablespoons dark soy sauce
2 tablespoons dry sherry
250 g (8 oz) spinach leaves, washed and shredded

Place the beans in a saucepan with plenty of cold water. Bring to the boil and boil rapidly for 10 minutes, then reduce the heat, cover and simmer for 1 hour or until the beans are tender. Drain, reserving 150 ml (¼ pint) of the cooking liquid.

Heat the oil in a large frying pan. Add the garlic, ginger and chillies and cook for 3 minutes. Add the mushrooms and cook for a further 5 minutes or until they are just tender.

Add the tomatoes, beans, reserved liquid, soy sauce and sherry. Bring the mix to the boil, cover and simmer for 15 minutes.

Stir in the spinach and heat through for 2–3 minutes until the spinach has wilted. Serve immediately.

103 Cannellini beans with leeks and rocket

104 Bean tagine

Preparation time:
10 minutes, plus soaking

Cooking time:
1 hour 20 minutes

Serves: **4–6**

125 g (4 oz) dried cannellini beans, soaked overnight, drained and rinsed
1.2 litres (2 pints) water
2 tablespoons walnut oil
2 leeks, trimmed and sliced
1 tablespoon mustard seeds
1 garlic clove, crushed
125 g (4 oz) French beans, trimmed and halved
75 ml (3 fl oz) double cream
125 g (4 oz) rocket
2 tablespoons snipped chives
salt and pepper

Preparation time:
15 minutes, plus soaking

Cooking time:
2½ hours

Oven temperature:
150°C (300°F) Gas Mark 2

Serves: **8**

500 g (1 lb) dried red or white kidney beans, soaked overnight and drained
2 celery sticks, halved
2 bay leaves
4 parsley sprigs
4 tablespoons olive oil
500 g (1 lb) onions, chopped
5 garlic cloves, crushed
2 red chillies, deseeded and chopped
4 red peppers, deseeded and chopped
1 tablespoon paprika
large handful of mixed chopped mint, parsley and coriander
salt and pepper
mint leaves, to garnish

TOMATO SAUCE:
1 kg (2 lb) canned chopped tomatoes
2 tablespoons olive oil
4 parsley sprigs
1 tablespoon sugar

Place the beans in a saucepan with the water. Bring to the boil and boil rapidly for 10 minutes. Reduce the heat and simmer gently for 45–50 minutes or until the beans are tender.

Strain the liquid from the beans into a pan and boil it rapidly until it has reduced to 300 ml (½ pint). Reserve.

Heat the oil in a saucepan and fry the leeks, mustard seeds and garlic for 5 minutes. Add the drained beans, French beans and reduced stock and simmer gently for 5 minutes until the French beans are tender. Remove from the heat. Strain the liquid into a small saucepan, add the cream and boil for 2–3 minutes until slightly reduced.

Stir the rocket and chives into the beans and drizzle the sauce over them. Season to taste and serve immediately.

Boil the beans in a large saucepan of unsalted water for 10 minutes then drain. Tie the celery, bay leaves and parsley together with kitchen string. Cover the beans with fresh unsalted water, add the celery and herbs and simmer for 1 hour or until the beans are just tender. Drain, reserving the cooking liquid. Discard the celery and herbs.

To make the tomato sauce, empty the tomatoes and their juice into a saucepan, add the oil, parsley and sugar and bring to the boil. Reduce the heat and simmer, uncovered, for about 20 minutes until thick.

Heat the oil in a flameproof casserole. Add the onion, garlic, chillies, red peppers and paprika and cook gently for 5 minutes. Stir in the beans, tomato sauce and enough of the reserved cooking liquid to cover the beans. Season, cover and cook in a preheated oven, 150°C (300°F), Gas Mark 2, for 1½ hours, stirring occasionally. Just before serving, stir in the mint, parsley and coriander. Garnish with mint leaves.

COOK'S NOTES Any dried beans could be used in this recipe if you can't get cannellini beans. Try red or white kidney beans, black-eyed beans, aduki beans or soya beans as a substitute.

105 Brown beans and egg

Preparation time:
8–10 minutes

Serves: **4**

425 g (14 oz) can brown beans, drained and rinsed
1 small pickled cucumber, roughly chopped
2 hard-boiled eggs, roughly chopped
salt and pepper
wholegrain bread, to serve

DRESSING:
2 garlic cloves, crushed
1 teaspoon cumin seeds
½ bunch of spring onions, finely sliced
small handful of parsley, chopped
1 tablespoon lemon juice
2 teaspoons harissa
4 tablespoons olive oil

First make the dressing. Mix together the garlic, cumin seeds, spring onions, parsley, lemon juice, harissa and oil in a large bowl.

In another bowl mix together the beans, cucumber and eggs. Season to taste. Toss together gently, transfer to the bowl of dressing and mix thoroughly. Serve with wholegrain bread.

COOK'S NOTES This dish makes a great starter or side salad. Health-food stores and delicatessens usually stock brown beans. Canned brown beans tend to be large, flattish and rather bland, hence this spiced, tangy dressing. Canned red kidney beans are a good substitute.

106 Mixed bean ratatouille

Preparation time:
10 minutes

Cooking time:
15 minutes

Serves:
4–6 as a side dish, 4 as a supper dish

175 g (6 oz) green beans, trimmed and halved
2 tablespoons vegetable oil
1 onion, finely chopped
2 garlic cloves, crushed
425 g (14 oz) can tomatoes
2 tablespoons tomato purée
1 teaspoon dried mixed herbs
¼–½ teaspoon sugar, according to taste
425 g (14 oz) can cannellini beans, drained and rinsed
2 tablespoons chopped basil, plus extra to garnish
salt and pepper

Blanch the green beans in a saucepan of lightly salted, boiling water for 2 minutes. Drain and rinse immediately under cold running water. Drain again and set aside.

Heat the oil in a saucepan. Add the onion and garlic and fry for 2–3 minutes or until softened but not browned.

Add the tomatoes. Use a wooden spoon to mix them with the onion and garlic and break them up. Add the tomato purée, dried herbs and sugar. Season to taste. Bring to the boil, stirring constantly.

Add the green beans and canned beans to the saucepan. Toss until the beans are piping hot and coated in the tomato sauce. Remove from the heat and stir in the basil. Check the seasoning and adjust if necessary. Serve immediately, garnished with basil.

Preparation time: **20 minutes**	**375 g (12 oz) shortcrust pastry, defrosted if frozen**
	1–2 tablespoons olive oil
Cooking time: **40–45 minutes**	**1 onion, finely chopped**
	1 large tomato, skinned, deseeded and chopped
Oven temperature: **200°C (400°F) Gas Mark 6, then 180°C (350°F) Gas Mark 4**	**4 basil leaves, finely chopped**
	8 baby courgettes, cut into wafer thin slices
	2 large eggs
	150 ml (¼ pint) double cream
	4 tablespoons grated mature Cheddar
Serves: **4**	**salt and pepper**

Divide the pastry into four and roll out into circles to line four 11 x 1.5 cm (4½ x ¾ inch) flan tins. Prick the bases gently with a fork. Put on a baking sheet and bake blind in a preheated oven, 200°C (400°F), Gas Mark 6, for 8–10 minutes. Carefully remove the baking beans and nonstick baking paper and bake for a further 8–10 minutes. Reduce the oven temperature to 180°C (350°F), Gas Mark 4.

Meanwhile, make the filling. Heat the oil in a frying pan. Add the onion and cook over a low heat for 5–10 minutes until soft but not coloured. Stir in the tomato and basil.

Spoon the filling into the cooked flan cases and arrange the courgette slices decoratively on top. Beat the eggs and cream together, season to taste and pour over the filling. Sprinkle with the grated cheese and cook in the oven for 20–25 minutes until just set and golden. Serve warm or cold.

Preparation time: **25 minutes**	**125 g (4 oz) plain flour**
	125 g (4 oz) wholemeal flour
	1 teaspoon salt
Cooking time: **50 minutes**	**50 g (2 oz) butter, softened**
	25 g (1 oz) lard or vegetable cooking fat
	about 5 tablespoons water
Oven temperature: **200°C (400°F) Gas Mark 6, then 180°C (350°F) Gas Mark 4**	**watercress sprigs, to garnish**
	FILLING:
	300 g (10 oz) ripe Brie
	300 ml (½ pint) milk
	125 g (4 oz) watercress, trimmed
Serves: **6**	**3 eggs, beaten**
	1 teaspoon mustard powder
	pepper

Sift the flours and salt into a bowl, adding the bran remaining in the sieve to the bowl. Rub in the fats until the mixture resembles breadcrumbs. Add just enough water to mix to a firm dough. Roll out the pastry on a lightly floured surface and use it to line a 23 cm (9 inch) loose-bottomed flan tin.

Prick the base all over with a fork and bake blind in a preheated oven, 200°C (400°F), Gas Mark 6, for 10 minutes. Remove from the oven. Reduce the oven temperature to 180°C (350°F), Gas Mark 4.

Meanwhile, make the filling. Remove the rind from the Brie. Dice the cheese, put it in a saucepan with the milk and stir over a low heat until blended. Remove from the heat, stir in the watercress, eggs and mustard and season with pepper to taste. Pour into the flan case and cook in the oven for 35–40 minutes. Allow to cool slightly before removing from the tin, then serve garnished with watercress.

COOK'S NOTES When you are making a flan case, keep the pastry in shape by filling it with crumpled foil or lining it with nonstick baking paper, weighed down with special baking beans. The foil or paper and beans are removed after the first baking. This is known as baking blind.

Preparation time: 15 minutes

Cooking time: 8–16 minutes

Serves: 4

2 packets of haloumi
1 bag of mixed lettuce
2 tablespoons olive oil
4 tablespoons lemon juice
1 bunch of marjoram, chopped
4 beef tomatoes, skinned, cored and cut into wedges
75 g (3 oz) pitted olives (optional)
salt and pepper

Heat a griddle pan until hot. Cut the haloumi into 16 slices and place on the griddle to cook for 3–4 minutes on each side.

Arrange the lettuce on four serving plates. Mix together the olive oil, lemon juice and marjoram and season to taste.

Arrange the haloumi and tomato wedges alternately on the lettuce. Add the olives, if using, and spoon over the dressing. Serve immediately, while the cheese is still warm.

COOK'S NOTES Haloumi is a Greek sheep's milk cheese with a firm texture similar to feta, which griddles very successfully.

Preparation time: 40 minutes

Cooking time: 40–50 minutes

Oven temperature: 200°C (400°F) Gas Mark 6, then 190°C (375°F) Gas Mark 5

Serves: 6

25 g (1 oz) butter
40 g (1½ oz) plain flour
1 teaspoon Dijon mustard
200 ml (7 fl oz) milk
50 g (2 oz) hard cheese, grated
4 eggs, separated
4 tablespoons chopped mixed herbs (basil, chervil, chives, tarragon, thyme)
salt and pepper

FILLING:
175 g (6 oz) ricotta or curd cheese
2 tablespoons olive oil
pinch of grated nutmeg
1 leek, finely chopped
750 g (1½ lb) fresh spinach, shredded

Grease a 23 x 33 cm (9 x 13 inch) Swiss roll tin and line with nonstick baking paper. Melt the butter in a saucepan, stir in the flour and mustard and cook over a low heat for 1 minute. Gradually stir in the milk. Bring the sauce slowly to the boil, stirring constantly. Cook over a low heat for 2 minutes. Remove the pan from the heat and leave to cool slightly, then beat in the cheese, egg yolks and herbs and season. Whisk the egg whites until stiff and fold them into the sauce.

Pour the mixture into the prepared tin and cook in a preheated oven, 200°C (400°F), Gas Mark 6, for 12–15 minutes until risen and firm to the touch. Remove from the oven and set aside to cool. Reduce the oven temperature to 190°C (375°F), Gas Mark 5. While the roulade is cooking, prepare the filling. Beat together the cheese and half the oil until smooth. Season with nutmeg and salt and pepper. Heat the remaining oil in a frying pan and fry the leek for 5 minutes. Add the spinach to the leeks and cook gently for 5 minutes more.

To assemble the roulade, turn the cooked base out of the tin and peel away the paper. Spread over the softened cheese and then the spinach mixture. Roll up from a short end and place on the oiled Swiss roll tin. Brush with oil and bake for 20–25 minutes. Serve hot, in slices.

111 Spinach pancakes

Preparation time: **15 minutes**	**125 g (4 oz) plain flour**
	½ teaspoon salt
	1 egg
Cooking time: **15–20 minutes**	**300 ml (½ pint) milk**
	1 tablespoon vegetable oil
	butter, for greasing
Makes: **8**	
	FILLING:
	250 g (8 oz) frozen spinach, defrosted
	125 g (4 oz) Cheddar, grated

Sift the flour and salt into a bowl and make a well in the centre. Add the egg and half the milk, stirring the ingredients with a wooden spoon and drawing the flour to the centre to make a smooth mixture. Beat in the remaining milk.

Lightly oil a 15 cm (6 inch) omelette pan and cook eight pancakes. Keep the cooked pancakes warm by stacking them between two large plates placed above a saucepan of simmering water. Lightly grease a flameproof dish.

To make the filling, cook the spinach according to the instructions on the packet. Drain thoroughly, squeezing out as much liquid as possible, and then chop finely.

Add half the grated cheese to the spinach, mix well and keep warm.

Divide the spinach mixture among the pancakes and roll them up. Place the pancakes in the prepared dish, sprinkle with the remaining cheese and grill quickly to brown. Serve hot.

112 Noodles with vegetables

Preparation time: **5 minutes**	**250 g (8 oz) dried egg noodles**
	2 tablespoons vegetable oil
	50 g (2 oz) leek, sliced
Cooking time: **about 10 minutes**	**25 g (1 oz) oyster mushrooms, torn**
	1 celery stick and leaf, chopped
	125 g (4 oz) Chinese leaves, sliced
Serves: **4**	**25 g (1 oz) cauliflower florets**
	2 tablespoons soy sauce
	1½ tablespoons sugar
	½ teaspoon salt
	1 teaspoon black pepper
	2 tablespoons crispy garlic
	fresh coriander leaves, to garnish

Cook the noodles in boiling water for 5–6 minutes or according to the instructions on the packet. Drain and rinse in cold water to prevent them from cooking further.

Heat the oil in a wok or large frying pan over a moderate heat, then add all of the ingredients one by one, including the noodles. Give a quick stir after each addition.

Stir-fry for 3–4 minutes, adding more oil if necessary. Check the seasoning. Serve immediately, garnished with coriander leaves.

COOK'S NOTES To make crispy garlic, simply slice some cloves of garlic and deep-fry the slices in groundnut oil until golden and crispy. Remove from the oil with a slotted spoon and drain on kitchen paper. Store in an airtight container until ready to use.

113 Vegetable moussaka

114 Baked squash with mascarpone and sage

Preparation time:
15 minutes

Cooking time:
about 2 hours

Oven temperature:
160°C (325°F)
Gas Mark 3

Serves: 4

50 g (2 oz) butter
3 tablespoons vegetable oil
2 aubergines, thinly sliced
4 potatoes, peeled and thinly sliced
3 large onions, chopped
2 garlic cloves, chopped
3 large tomatoes, skinned and sliced
salt and pepper

CHEESE SAUCE:
50 g (2 oz) butter
40 g (1½ oz) wholemeal flour
600 ml (1 pint) milk
250 g (8 oz) Cheddar, grated
½–1 teaspoon grated nutmeg
1 teaspoon French mustard

Preparation time:
10–15 minutes

Cooking time:
1 hour 5 minutes

Oven temperature:
200°C (400°F)
Gas Mark 6

Serves: 4

2 small acorn squash,
each about 500 g (1 lb)
2 tablespoons olive oil
2 garlic cloves, crushed
2 tablespoons chopped sage
175 g (6 oz) mascarpone
4 sun-dried tomatoes in oil, drained
and chopped
2 tablespoons freshly grated Parmesan
salt and pepper

TO SERVE:
grilled bread
green salad

Heat half the butter and oil in a frying pan, add the aubergines and potatoes in batches and cook for 10 minutes, turning once. Remove from the pan.

Heat the rest of the butter and oil, add the onions, garlic and tomatoes and cook for 10 minutes; make sure they do nor brown. Mix half the aubergines and potatoes with the tomato mixture and season to taste. Reserve the rest of the aubergines and potatoes to make the topping.

To make the sauce, heat the butter, add the flour and stir over moderate heat for 1–2 minutes. Gradually blend in the milk. Stir to make a smooth sauce, remove from the heat, then add about 175 g (6 oz) of the cheese and the nutmeg and mustard. Season to taste.

Spoon half of the mixed vegetables into a casserole, add half of the sauce and the remainder of the mixed vegetables. Top with a neat layer of aubergines and potatoes, then the remaining sauce.

Cover the casserole with a lid. Bake in a preheated oven, 160°C (325°F), Gas Mark 3, for 1¼ hours. Remove the lid, add the remaining cheese, return to the oven, raising the heat slightly, and cook for a further 10 minutes or until the cheese topping has melted.

Cut the squash in half lengthways and carefully scoop out the seeds. Season the shells lightly and place them, cut sides up, in a roasting tin. Drizzle over a little of the oil and bake in a preheated oven, 200°C (400°F), Gas Mark 6, for 45 minutes.

Heat the oil in a frying pan and gently fry the garlic and sage for 4–5 minutes or until the garlic is softened.

Remove the squash from the oven and fill the hollows with the garlic mixture. Spoon in the mascarpone and scatter over the sun-dried tomatoes and Parmesan. Return to the oven for 15–20 minutes or until it is bubbling and golden. Serve with some grilled bread and a crisp green salad.

COOK'S NOTES Little Gem or other types of squash can be used in this recipe if you can't find acorn squash.

115 Aubergine and red pepper bake

116 Ratatouille

Preparation time: **15 minutes**	**3 red peppers, halved lengthways and deseeded, leaving the cores intact**
	2 aubergines, each sliced into 12 rounds
Cooking time: **30 minutes**	**1 tablespoon oil**
	250 g (8 oz) fresh paglia e fieno
	2 tablespoons pesto
Oven temperature: **180°C (350°F) Gas Mark 4**	**150 ml (¼ pint) single cream**
	10 black olives, pitted and quartered
	250 g (8 oz) feta, crumbled
	salt and pepper
Serves: **6**	**rocket leaves, to garnish**
	1 tablespoon lime juice, to serve

Put the pepper halves on a baking sheet and cook in a preheated oven, 180°C (350°F), Gas Mark 4, for 15 minutes. While they are cooking, arrange the aubergine slices on a grill rack, brush with oil and place under a preheated grill for 5 minutes until crisp. Turn, brush with oil and cook on the other side.

Bring at least 1.8 litres (3 pints) of water to the boil in a large saucepan. Add a dash of oil and a generous pinch of salt. Cook the pasta for 3 minutes until just tender. Drain the pasta and return to the pan with the pesto, cream and black olives. Season generously.

Remove the peppers from the oven. Place 2 cooked aubergine slices on an oiled baking sheet. Sit a pepper half on top. Put some feta into the pepper then carefully fill with some pasta. Crumble a little more feta over the pasta and top with two more aubergine rounds. Sprinkle with more feta. Repeat with the remaining ingredients, making six in all. Drizzle with a little oil and cook in a preheated oven, 180°C (350°F), Gas Mark 4, for 15 minutes.

To serve, sprinkle with a little lime juice and garnish with rocket leaves.

COOK'S NOTES Paglia e fieno are fine green and white noodles. If you can't find them, use fresh linguine or tagliatelle instead.

Preparation time: **10 minutes**	**125 ml (4 fl oz) olive oil**
	2 large aubergines, quartered lengthways and cut into 1 cm (½ inch) slices
Cooking time: **30 minutes**	**2 courgettes, cut into 1 cm (½ inch) slices**
	2 large red peppers, cored, deseeded and cut into squares
Oven temperature: **220°C (425°F) Gas Mark 7**	**1 large yellow pepper, cored, deseeded and cut into squares**
	2 large onions, thinly sliced
Serves: **8–9**	**3 large garlic cloves, crushed**
	1 tablespoon double-concentrate tomato purée
	400 g (13 oz) can plum tomatoes
	12 basil leaves, chopped
	1 tablespoon finely chopped marjoram or oregano
	1 teaspoon finely chopped thyme
	1 tablespoon paprika
	2–4 tablespoons finely chopped parsley
	salt and pepper

Heat half the oil in a roasting tin in a preheated oven, 220°C (425°F), Gas Mark 7. Add the aubergines, courgettes and peppers, toss in the hot oil, return to the oven and roast for about 30 minutes or until the vegetables are tender.

Meanwhile, heat the remaining oil in a deep saucepan. Add the onions and garlic and fry over a medium heat, stirring occasionally, for 5–10 minutes until soft but not coloured. Add the tomato purée, plum tomatoes, basil, marjoram or oregano, thyme and paprika. Season to taste. Stir to combine the ingredients, then cook for 10–15 minutes until the mixture is thick and syrupy.

Use a slotted spoon to transfer the vegetables from the roasting tin to the tomato mixture. Gently stir to combine, then add the parsley. Check the seasoning. Serve hot or cooled to room temperature.

6   Fish Dishes

117 Smoky chillied prawns

118 Tiger prawns with mint and lemon

Preparation time: **15 minutes, plus marinating**	**10 green chillies, halved lengthways and deseeded**
	20 raw king prawns, peeled with the tails left on
Cooking time: **6 minutes**	**5 tablespoons olive oil**
	coarsely ground sea salt
	lemon wedges, to serve
Serves: **4**	

Preparation time: **10 minutes, plus marinating time**	**750 g (1½ lb) raw tiger prawns peeled and deveined**
	1 large bunch of mint, chopped
	2 garlic cloves, crushed
Cooking time: **4–6 minutes**	**8 tablespoons lemon juice**
	salt and pepper
	mint leaves, to garnish
Serves: **4**	

Wrap one half of each chilli round the middle of a prawn then thread 5 prawns on to each of four metal or bamboo skewers.

Place the skewers in a long, shallow dish and sprinkle over the oil and sea salt. Cover the dish and leave to marinate in a cool place for about 30 minutes.

Cook the prawns on the oiled grill of a preheated barbecue or under a preheated grill for 3 minutes on each side, basting with any remaining marinade. Serve the prawns hot with lemon wedges.

Place the prawns in a glass mixing bowl. Add the mint, garlic and lemon juice to the prawns, season to taste and allow to marinate for 30 minutes or overnight.

Heat a griddle pan until hot. Place the prawns and marinade on the griddle, cook for 2–3 minutes on each side and serve garnished with mint leaves.

COOK'S NOTES If you are using bamboo skewers, soak them in water for 30 minutes before threading on the prawns, to prevent them burning during cooking.

COOK'S NOTES Serve this fresh-flavoured dish as a starter with some crusty bread to mop up the juices, or as a main course accompanied by new potatoes and buttered asparagus.

119 Stir-fried prawns

Preparation time: 20 minutes	**4 tablespoons vegetable oil**
	15 g (½ oz) fresh root ginger, peeled and cut into matchstick strips
Cooking time: 5–7 minutes	**2 garlic cloves, chopped**
	8 spring onions, sliced diagonally
	1 carrot, cut into matchstick strips
Serves: **4**	**8 celery sticks, sliced diagonally**
	375 g (12 oz) cauliflower, separated into tiny florets
	2 red peppers, cored, deseeded and diced
	1 green pepper, cored, deseeded and thinly shredded
	1 kg (2 lb) large raw peeled prawns
	celery leaves, to garnish

GLAZE:
2 teaspoons cornflour
6 tablespoons water
2 tablespoons white wine vinegar
2 teaspoons soy sauce
2 teaspoons tomato purée
salt and pepper

Heat the oil in a wok or large frying pan, add the ginger and garlic and stir-fry over a moderate heat for 30 seconds. Add the spring onions, carrot and celery and stir-fry for 1 minute, then add the cauliflower and stir-fry for 30 seconds. Add the red and green peppers and stir-fry for a further 30 seconds. Add the prawns and cook for 2–3 minutes.

Mix together all the glaze ingredients in a bowl, pour them into the pan and stir over brisk heat until all the prawns and vegetables are coated. Turn on to warmed plates, garnish with the celery leaves and serve immediately.

120 Kerala prawn curry

Preparation time: 5 minutes	**½ teaspoon ground turmeric**
	500 g (1 lb) large prawns, cooked and peeled
Cooking time: 8 minutes	**1 teaspoon vegetable oil**
	1 red onion, cut into fine wedges
	2 green chillies, deseeded and sliced
Serves: **4**	**10 curry leaves (optional)**
	100 ml (3½ fl oz) coconut milk
	2 tablespoons lime juice
	2 tablespoons coriander leaves
	salt and pepper

Sprinkle the turmeric over the prawns and set aside. Heat the oil in a wok and stir-fry the onion wedges and chillies until they are softened.

Add the prawns, curry leaves (if using) and coconut milk. Simmer for 5 minutes.

Sprinkle over the lime juice and season to taste. Scatter with coriander leaves and stir once. Serve immediately.

121 Sichuan scallops

122 Seared scallops with lime dressing

Preparation time:	2 tablespoons oil
15 minutes	750 g (1½ lb) scallops
	2 garlic cloves, crushed
Cooking time:	1 dried red chilli, finely chopped
6 minutes	½ teaspoon Chinese five-spice powder
	2.5 cm (1 inch) fresh root ginger, peeled
Serves: 4	and finely shredded
	2 tablespoons Chinese wine
	2 tablespoons dark soy sauce
	3 tablespoons water
	6 spring onions, diagonally sliced
	1 small onion, sliced
	1 teaspoon caster sugar
	2 spring onions, shredded, to garnish

Heat the oil in a wok or large frying pan until smoking hot. Add the scallops and sear on both sides, remove and reserve.

Add the garlic, chilli, Chinese five-spice powder and ginger and stir-fry for 1 minute. Add the Chinese wine, soy sauce, water, spring onions, onion and caster sugar and stir-fry for 1 minute then return the scallops to the wok and stir-fry them in the sauce for 2 minutes.

Arrange the scallops with their sauce on a warmed serving dish and garnish with the spring onions.

Preparation time:	16 large scallops
10 minutes	grated rind and juice of 2 limes
	3 tablespoons olive oil
Cooking time:	bunch of dill, chopped
4 minutes	salt and pepper
	large bag of mixed leaves, to serve
Serves: 4	

Heat a griddle pan until hot. Dry the scallops thoroughly with kitchen paper to remove excess water and place them on the hot griddle. Cook for 2 minutes on each side.

Mix together the lime juice and rind, olive oil and chopped dill. Season to taste.

Toss the salad in the lime dressing and arrange it on four plates. Place the scallops on the salad and serve with a little dressing.

COOK'S NOTES Don't cook the scallops in the sauce for any more than 2 minutes or they will become tough. Scallops should be served only just cooked, to keep them tender and sweet.

123 Ceviche

124 Squid with herbs

Preparation time: **15 minutes, plus marinating**	**500 g (1 lb) mixed seafood (such as fillets of sole, flounder, haddock, scallops and prawns)**
	125 ml (4 fl oz) lime juice
Serves: **4**	**2 tomatoes, skinned, deseeded and chopped**
	½ teaspoon dried red chilli flakes
	1 tablespoon olive oil
	½ teaspoon salt
	pinch of dried oregano
	pepper
	2 limes, cut into wedges, to garnish

Clean and rinse the fish in cold water and pat it dry with kitchen paper. Cut the fish and scallops into thin slices. Peel and devein the prawns.

Put all the fish in a ceramic bowl and pour the lime juice over the top, making sure all the fish pieces are well coated in the juice. Cover with clingflim and chill in the refrigerator for 3–4 hours or until the fish has become opaque.

Stir the tomatoes, chilli flakes, olive oil, salt, oregano and pepper into the chilled fish. Mix well and refrigerate for another 2–3 hours. Allow to stand at room temperature for 15 minutes before serving, then garnish with lime wedges.

Preparation time: **10 minutes**	**1 kg (2 lb) prepared baby squid**
	4 tablespoons olive oil
	3–4 garlic cloves, thickly sliced
Cooking time: **2 minutes**	**2 tablespoons chopped thyme**
	1 tablespoon chopped parsley
	juice of ½ lemon
Serves: **4**	**salt and pepper**
	lemon wedges, to garnish

Score the squid in a criss-cross pattern and cut the tentacles in half if they are large. Heat the oil in a wok or large frying pan, add the garlic and cook gently until browned, then discard. Season the squid.

Increase the heat, add the squid to the wok and cook briskly for just under 1 minute. Sprinkle with the herbs and lemon juice. Serve immediately, garnished with the lemon wedges.

TIP If you need to prepare squid yourself, draw back the rim of the body pouch to locate the quill-shaped pen and pull it out. Gently pull the body from the tentacles just below the eyes – the inedible head and ink sac will come away together. Slip a finger under the skin and peel it off.

125 Catalan mussels

126 Moules marinière

Preparation time:	**1 tablespoon olive oil**
10 minutes	**1 onion, finely chopped**
	2 garlic cloves, crushed
Cooking time:	**1 red chilli, deseeded and finely chopped**
15 minutes	**pinch of paprika**
	400 g (13 oz) can chopped tomatoes
Serves: **4**	**1 kg (2 lb) mussels**
	salt and pepper
	parsley, chopped, to garnish

Preparation time:	**65 g (2½ oz) butter**
15 minutes	**4 shallots, finely chopped**
	1 garlic clove, crushed
Cooking time:	**350 ml (12 fl oz) white wine**
20 minutes	**1 bouquet garni**
	2 kg (4 lb) fresh mussels
Serves: **4–6**	**2 tablespoons chopped parsley**
	salt and pepper
	strips of lemon rind, to garnish

Heat the oil in a large saucepan or wok. Fry the onion, garlic, chilli and paprika over a medium heat for 10 minutes or until soft. Stir in the tomatoes and season. Cover and simmer over a low heat while you prepare the mussels.

Stir the cleaned mussels into the tomato sauce, increase the heat and cover with a lid. Cook for 5 minutes until the shells have opened. Discard any mussels that remain closed.

Pile into warmed serving bowls, sprinkle with the parsley and serve.

Melt the butter in a large saucepan, stir in the shallots and garlic and fry gently until soft. Stir in the wine and then add the bouquet garni and bring to the boil. Boil for 2 minutes and season to taste.

Add the mussels, cover the pan and cook over a high heat, shaking vigorously from time to time, until the mussel shells open. Remove the mussels from the pan with a slotted spoon and set them aside, discarding any that have not opened.

Boil the liquid rapidly until it is reduced by half, then return the mussels to the pan and heat through for 1 minute, shaking the pan constantly. Sprinkle with the parsley and shake the pan again. Pile the mussels in a deep, warmed serving dish or in individual serving dishes and pour the liquid over the top. Garnish with the lemon rind and serve immediately.

COOK'S NOTES To prepare the mussels, pull off the beards and scrub the shells with a small brush. Discard any that remain open after you have tapped them on the work surface, or any that are broken.

127 Mussels with Thai herbs

128 Quick shellfish stew

Preparation time:	**2 kg (4 lb) fresh mussels**
20 minutes	**1.2 litres (2 pints) water**
	6 kaffir lime leaves or ½ teaspoon grated
Cooking time:	**lime rind**
20 minutes	**rind of 1 lemon**
	2 lemon grass stalks
Serves: **4**	**1 tablespoon salt**
	3 red chillies, sliced
	3 spring onions, chopped
	coriander leaves, to garnish

Pour the water into a large saucepan and bring to the boil. Add the lime leaves or lime rind, lemon rind, lemon grass and salt. Add the mussels, cover the pan and bring back to the boil.

Cook the mussels, shaking the pan occasionally, until they open. Drain them, reserving half the cooking liquid. Transfer the mussels to a deep serving dish, discarding any that have not opened.

Strain the reserved liquid, discarding the lime leaves or lime rind, lemon rind and lemon grass. Bring to the boil, add the sliced red chillies and spring onions, and boil vigorously for about 2–3 minutes. Pour the sauce over the mussels and serve immediately, garnished with coriander leaves.

Preparation time:	**4 shallots, chopped**
5 minutes	**2 celery sticks, finely chopped**
	125 ml (4 fl oz) white wine
Cooking time:	**1 tablespoon chopped mixed herbs**
25 minutes	**400 g (13 oz) can plum tomatoes**
	500 g (1 lb) mixed shellfish (such as
Serves: **4**	**scallops, mussels, tiger prawns,**
	langoustines and lobster tails)
	2 tablespoons chopped dill

Dry-fry the shallots and celery in a nonstick saucepan for 1 minute or until they are just starting to soften. Add the wine and allow the mixture to sizzle and reduce by half. Add the mixed herbs.

Stir in the tomatoes with their juice. Use a wooden spoon to break up the tomatoes and cook for 5 minutes to reduce and thicken the juice. Add the shellfish and half the dill. Stir once, cover with a lid and simmer for 10 minutes. Season and garnish with the remaining chopped dill.

COOK'S NOTES Be sure to cut the larger shellfish, such as lobster tails, into smaller pieces so they cook at the same rate as the other shellfish. Alternatively, put them into the sauce a couple of minutes before the smaller items.

129 Crab-stuffed tortillas

Preparation time:
10 minutes

Cooking time:
30–35 minutes

Oven temperature:
200°C (400°F)
Gas Mark 6

Serves: **4–6**

oil, for shallow-frying
12 soft corn tortillas
500 g (1 lb) crabmeat
250 g (8 oz) Cheddar, grated
125 g (4 oz) mozzarella, diced
1 small red onion, finely chopped
guacamole, to serve

RED CHILLI SAUCE:
5 small dried red chillies, crumbled
425 g (14 oz) can chopped tomatoes,
drained (reserve the juice)
4 tablespoons oil
2 onions, chopped
2 garlic cloves, crushed
3 tablespoons tomato purée
1 teaspoon ground cumin
1 teaspoon ground coriander
1½ tablespoons wine vinegar
1 teaspoon sugar

First make the chilli sauce. Purée the chillies in a food processor or blender with the tomatoes and 3 tablespoons boiling water to make a smooth paste. Heat the oil in a saucepan and cook the onions and garlic until they are soft. Stir in the chilli and tomato mixture, the reserved tomato juice, the tomato purée, cumin, coriander, vinegar and sugar. Cover the pan and simmer for 10 minutes.

Heat the oil in a frying pan and shallow-fry the tortillas one at a time over a moderate heat for a few seconds until they become limp. Pat the tortillas with kitchen paper and spread each one with a little chilli sauce. Put some crabmeat in the centre of each one. Sprinkle some Cheddar and mozzarella on top, reserving a little, and some chopped onion. Roll up the tortillas and arrange them in a buttered ovenproof dish. Pour over the remaining chilli sauce and scatter with the rest of the cheese. Bake in a preheated oven, 200°C (400°F), Gas Mark 6, for 15–20 minutes. Serve with guacamole.

130 Griddled tuna with parsnip purée

Preparation time:
15 minutes

Cooking time:
15 minutes

Serves: **4**

4 tuna steaks, each about 125 g (4 oz)
2 teaspoons olive oil
steamed green vegetables, to serve
(optional)

GLAZE:
1 tablespoon honey
2 tablespoons wholegrain mustard
1 teaspoon tomato purée
2 tablespoons orange juice
1 tablespoon red wine vinegar or
balsamic vinegar
pepper

PARSNIP PURÉE:
2 parsnips, cut into chunks
2 potatoes, cut into chunks
50 g (2 oz) natural yogurt
2 teaspoons horseradish relish (optional)

First make the glaze. Put the ingredients in a small saucepan, bring them to the boil, then reduce the heat and simmer until the mixture reduces and is of a glaze consistency. Keep hot.

Next make the parsnip purée. Steam the parsnips and potatoes until they are tender. Drain if necessary and place in a food processor or blender with the yogurt, horseradish (if using) and pepper to taste. Process until blended. Keep warm or reheat before serving.

Brush the tuna with oil. Cook on a preheated, very hot griddle or barbecue, in a frying pan or under a grill for 1–2 minutes. Turn and spoon the glaze over the tuna. Cook for a further 1–2 minutes but do not overcook because tuna is best when it is moist and still slightly pink in the centre.

To serve, top a mound of the purée with a tuna steak and spoon over the remaining glaze. Serve with steamed green vegetables, if liked.

Preparation time:	4 tuna steaks, each about 125 g (4 oz)
5 minutes	50 g (2 oz) plain flour
	4 tablespoons olive oil
Cooking time:	1 small onion, finely chopped
25 minutes	4 parsley sprigs, finely chopped
	125 ml (4 fl oz) dry white wine
Serves: 4	1 tablespoon capers, drained
	1 bay leaf, crumbled
	¼ teaspoon ground cinnamon
	salt and pepper

TO SERVE:
new potatoes
green salad

Coat the tuna steaks in flour. Heat the oil in a large frying pan, mix together the onion and parsley and add them to the pan. Cook over a moderate heat, stirring, until they are just golden but not brown.

Add the tuna steaks and cook for 2 minutes on each side. Season to taste and add the wine. Wait until the wine has evaporated a little, then add the capers, crumbled bay leaf and cinnamon. Cover and cook for 15 minutes, adding extra water if needed.

Serve the tuna steaks with the cooking juices poured over, accompanied by new potatoes and a green salad.

Preparation time:	4–6 tablespoons oil
15–20 minutes	2–3 garlic cloves, crushed
	1 large onion, finely chopped
Cooking time:	150 g (5 oz) button mushrooms, quartered
about 1 hour	or thickly sliced
	6–8 anchovy fillets, chopped
Oven temperature:	2 tablespoons chopped parsley
190°C (375°F)	1 tablespoon plain flour
Gas Mark 5	300 ml (10 fl oz) dry white wine
	pepper
Serves: 4	pinch) of nutmeg
	4 tuna steaks, each about 150 g (5 oz) and
	about 1 cm (½ inch) thick

Heat the oil in a pan and cook the garlic and onion until soft and lightly coloured. Add the mushrooms and cook for a further 2–3 minutes, then add the anchovies, parsley and flour. Mix the ingredients together.

Stir in the wine, bring to the boil, stirring all the time, then simmer gently for 5–7 minutes.

Season to taste with pepper and a pinch of nutmeg. There should be no need to add salt because anchovies are already salty.

Place the tuna steaks in an oven-to-table dish and pour over the sauce.

Cover with a lid or foil and cook in a preheated oven, 190°C (375°F), Gas Mark 5, for 40–45 minutes. Serve hot.

COOK'S NOTES Capers, which are usually pickled in vinegar, are the small unopened flowerbuds of a Mediterranean plant. They add a piquant flavour to sauces, dressings and salads and go especially well with fish.

COOK'S NOTES Swordfish or halibut steaks would be equally successful in this recipe, instead of tuna.

133 Thai fishcakes

134 Salmon fishcakes

Preparation time:
15 minutes

Cooking time:
15 minutes

Serves: **4**

500 g (1 lb) fish fillets, cooked (such as salmon, cod or haddock)
1 garlic clove, crushed
2.5 cm (1 inch) fresh root ginger, peeled and finely diced
2 red chillies, chopped
1 bunch of coriander, chopped
2 teaspoons Thai fish sauce
1 egg yolk
250 g (8 oz) mashed potatoes
oil, for shallow-frying

Flake the fish, removing any bones, and place it in a blender or food processor with the garlic, ginger, chillies, coriander, fish sauce and egg yolk. Process well until smooth.

Remove the fish mixture from the processor or blender and use a fork to mix it thoroughly with the mashed potatoes. Shape the mixture into 12 cakes (or 24 smaller ones), dusting your hands with flour if the mixture is sticky.

Heat the oil in a frying pan, add the fishcakes and fry for 2–3 minutes on each side or until golden-brown and heated through.

Preparation time:
30–35 minutes, plus chilling

Cooking time:
about 12 minutes

Serves: **4**

300 g (10 oz) potatoes, boiled in their skins then peeled
25 g (1 oz) butter or margarine
300 g (10 oz) salmon fillet, cooked
2 tablespoons chopped parsley
2 eggs, beaten
75 g (3 oz) dry breadcrumbs
oil, for shallow-frying
salt and pepper
chives, to garnish
tomato salad, to serve

Mash the potatoes in a bowl with the butter or margarine, then mix in the salmon, parsley and half the beaten egg. Season to taste, cover and chill for 20 minutes.

Place the salmon mixture on a floured surface and shape it into a roll. Cut it into eight slices and shape each one into a flat cake, about 6 cm (2½ inches) in diameter. Dip each fishcake into the remaining beaten egg and coat with breadcrumbs.

Heat the oil in a frying pan, add the fishcakes and fry for 2–3 minutes on each side or until golden-brown and heated through. Garnish with chives and serve with a tomato salad.

COOK'S NOTES These fishcakes can also be cooked in a preheated griddle pan without oil. Allow about 2–3 minutes on each side.

135 Salmon steaks in fresh coriander sauce

136 Salmon and potato parcels

Preparation time:	**4 salmon steaks, each 175–250 g (6–8 oz)**
10 minutes	**125 g (4 oz) unsalted butter, plus extra for greasing**
Cooking time:	**½ onion, finely chopped**
40 minutes	**1 carrot, cut into matchstick strips**
	1 garlic clove, finely chopped
Oven temperature:	**1 bay leaf**
190°C (375°F)	**1 tablespoon dry vermouth (optional)**
Gas Mark 5	**125 ml (4 fl oz) Fish Stock (see introduction)**
Serves: **4**	**1 bunch of coriander, finely chopped**
	125 ml (4 fl oz) double cream
	1–2 tablespoons lemon juice
	salt and pepper
	lime wedges, to garnish
	steamed vegetables, to serve

Rinse the salmon steaks in cold water, pat them dry on kitchen paper and season to taste.

Melt half the butter in a small frying pan. Add the onion and carrot and cook over a low heat for 4–5 minutes. Add the garlic and cook for a further 2 minutes.

Pour into a shallow ovenproof dish, add the bay leaf then arrange the fish on top in a single layer. Sprinkle with vermouth, if using, then with the fish stock. Cover with buttered foil and bake in a preheated oven, 190°C (375°F), Gas Mark 5, for 20–25 minutes, depending on the thickness of the fish. It should just flake easily when tested with a fork. Remove the fish to a warmed serving plate and keep warm.

Strain the cooking juices into a clean pan and boil vigorously for 1–2 minutes to reduce. Add half the remaining butter, the coriander and the cream and simmer for 4–5 minutes until the sauce is slightly thickened. Add the lemon juice, stir for 1 minute, add the remaining butter and whisk until it is smooth and glossy. Adjust the seasoning if necessary, then pour the sauce over the fish, garnish with the lime wedges and serve with vegetables.

Preparation time:	**15 g (½ oz) butter**
25 minutes	**½ onion, finely chopped**
	¼ teaspoon fennel seeds, roughly ground
Cooking time:	**1 teaspoon finely grated lemon rind**
35–40 minutes	**250 g (8 oz) potatoes, peeled and boiled**
	1 tablespoon chopped dill
Oven temperature:	**175 g (6 oz) smoked salmon, chopped**
220°C (425°F)	**1 tablespoon lemon juice**
Gas Mark 7	**1 egg yolk**
	500 g (1 lb) puff pastry, defrosted if frozen
Makes: **8**	**flour, for dusting**
	salt and pepper

EGG GLAZE:
1 small egg
1 tablespoon milk
pinch of salt

Melt the butter in a small saucepan and fry the onion, fennel seeds and lemon rind for 10 minutes or until very soft. Transfer to a bowl.

Mash the cooked potatoes with fork so that they are still fairly coarse. Add the potatoes to the onion in the bowl together with the dill, smoked salmon, lemon juice and egg yolk and mix until thoroughly blended. Season to taste.

Roll out the puff pastry on a lightly floured surface to form a thin rectangle, 17 x 34 cm (7 x 14 inches). Cut it into 8 squares, each measuring 8.5 cm (3½ inches).

Divide the filling among the pastry squares, placing a mound of filling slightly off-centre on each square. Dampen the edges of the pastry and fold each one in half diagonally to form a triangle. Press the edges together to seal.

Transfer the pastry triangles to a lightly greased baking sheet. Beat together the ingredients for the egg glaze and brush the glaze lightly over the pastry. Bake in a preheated oven, 220°C (425°F), Gas Mark 7, for 15–20 minutes until the pastry is puffed up and golden. Serve hot.

137 Salmon wrapped in Parma ham

138 Baked cod steaks and tomato sauce

Preparation time: **10 minutes**	**4 salmon fillets, each about 175 g (6 oz), skinned** **4 thin slices of Fontina**
Cooking time: **10 minutes**	**4 – 8 bay leaves, depending on size** **8 thin slices of Parma ham** **salt and pepper**
Serves: **4**	**fresh pasta or mixed salad leaves, to serve**

Heat a griddle pan until hot. Season the salmon fillets to taste.

Trim any rind from the Fontina and cut it to fit on top of the salmon fillets. Place the cheese slices on the salmon fillets, then place the bay leaves on top of the cheese and wrap the Parma ham around the salmon, securing the cheese and bay leaves with the ham.

Cook the prepared salmon fillets on the griddle for 4–5 minutes on each side, taking care when turning that you do not spill the fish or cheese.

Serve with fresh pasta tossed in butter, or a leafy salad.

Preparation time: **7 minutes, plus cooling**	**400 g (13 oz) can chopped tomatoes** **1 garlic clove, crushed** **2 tablespoons olive oil, plus extra for brushing**
Cooking time: **1 hour 20 minutes**	**1 teaspoon chopped thyme** **1 teaspoon grated lemon rind** **pinch of sugar**
Oven temperature: **200°C (400°F) Gas Mark 6**	**2 tablespoons chopped basil** **4 cod steaks, each about 175 g (6 oz), washed and dried** **50 g (2 oz) pitted black olives**
Serves: **4**	**250 g (8 oz) mozzarella, thinly sliced** **salt and pepper** **basil sprigs, to garnish**

Place the tomatoes, garlic, olive oil, thyme, lemon rind, sugar and seasoning in a small saucepan. Bring to the boil over a low heat, cover and simmer for 30 minutes. Remove the lid from the pan and cook for a further 15 minutes or until the sauce is thick. Stir in the basil and set aside to cool.

Place the cod steaks in a shallow, oiled ovenproof dish. Pour over the tomato sauce and scatter over the olives. Place the slices of cheese over the fish so they are completely covered.

Cover the dish loosely with foil and bake in a preheated oven, 200°C (400°F), Gas Mark 6, for 20 minutes. Remove the foil and bake for a further 10–15 minutes until the cheese is bubbling and golden and the fish is cooked through. Garnish with basil sprigs and serve immediately.

COOK'S NOTES Fontina is a full-fat Italian cheese with an orange rind and a nutty flavour. It melts easily and adds a lovely creamy quality to the dish.

139 Masala roast cod

140 Cod steaks with mint pesto

Preparation time:
15 minutes

Cooking time:
30 minutes

Oven temperature:
200°C (400°F)
Gas Mark 6

Serves: **4**

1 red chilli, chopped
2 garlic cloves, chopped
1 teaspoon minced ginger
1 teaspoon mustard seeds
large pinch of turmeric
2 cloves
2 cardamoms
5 peppercorns
3 tablespoons water
1 teaspoon olive oil
3 tablespoons natural yogurt
25 g (1 oz) breadcrumbs
500 g (1 lb) cod fillet
250 g (8 oz) ripe tomatoes, chopped

TO GARNISH:
lemon wedges
coriander leaves

Preparation time:
10 minutes

Cooking time:
8–10 minutes

Serves: **4**

4 cod steaks, each about 175 g (6 oz)
steamed green vegetables, to serve
1 lime, cut into wedges, to garnish

MINT PESTO:
6 tablespoons chopped mint
1 tablespoon chopped parsley
1 garlic clove, crushed
1 tablespoon freshly grated Parmesan
1 tablespoon double cream
1 teaspoon balsamic vinegar
3 tablespoons olive oil
salt and pepper
lime wedges, to garnish
steamed green vegetables, to serve

Put the chilli, garlic, ginger, mustard seeds, turmeric, cloves, cardamoms, peppercorns and water into a coffee grinder and blend to form a paste. Alternatively, use a pestle and mortar.

Heat the oil in a small pan and fry the chilli paste until the oil comes to the surface. Remove from the heat and stir in the yogurt and breadcrumbs.

Place the cod in an ovenproof dish and spread the chilli paste over it. Scatter over the tomatoes and cook, covered, in a preheated oven, 200°C (400°F), Gas Mark 6, for 30 minutes or until the fish is tender. Garnish with lemon wedges and coriander leaves.

Heat a griddle pan until hot, put on the cod steaks and cook for 4 minutes on each side, until the fish is slightly charred and firm to the touch.

Next make the pesto. Put all the ingredients in a blender or food processor and process until smooth then transfer to a small bowl.

Serve the cod steaks with a spoonful of pesto and seasonal steamed green vegetables, and garnished with lime wedges.

COOK'S NOTES Serve the fish with a mound of boiled rice which has been tossed with chopped coriander and grated lemon rind.

Preparation time: **10 minutes**	**4 cod fillets, each about 125 g (4 oz)** **50 g (2 oz) wholemeal breadcrumbs** **2 tablespoons chopped dill**
Cooking time: **20 minutes**	**2 tablespoons chopped parsley** **2 tablespoons chopped chives** **2 tablespoons fromage frais**
Oven temperature: **180°C (350°F)** **Gas Mark 4**	**2 plum tomatoes, finely diced** **2 tablespoons lemon juice** **salt and pepper**

Serves: **4**

Wipe the cod fillets with kitchen paper and season with salt and pepper. Put them in a foil-lined roasting tin, skin side down.

Mix together the remaining ingredients in a bowl and spoon some on top of each cod fillet, packing it down gently.

Cook in a preheated oven, 180°C (350°F), Gas Mark 4, for 20 minutes, covering with foil if the crust is over-browning, and serve immediately.

Preparation time: **30 minutes**	**25 g (1 oz) butter or margarine** **1 onion, sliced** **40 g (1½ oz) plain flour**
Cooking time: **1–1 1/4 hours**	**300 ml (½ pint dry cider** **2 leeks, trimmed and sliced**

Oven temperature: **180°C (350°F)**
Gas Mark 4
	375 g (12 oz) cooking apples, peeled,
	  cored and sliced
	750 g (1½ lb) haddock fillets, skinned and
	  thickly sliced
	salt and pepper

Serves: **4**

TO GARNISH:

1 apple, peeled, cored and sliced
1 teaspoon oil, to grill the apple rings
1 tablespoon chopped parsley

Melt the butter or margarine in a saucepan and cook the onion over a moderate heat for 10 minutes but do not let the onion brown. Stir in the flour and cook for 2 minutes.

Add the cider, bring to the boil and cook for 3 minutes, stirring until thickened. Season well.

Place the leeks, apple slices and fish in a shallow 1.8 litre/3 pint ovenproof dish. Pour over the sauce. Cover and cook in a preheated oven, 180°C (350°F), Gas Mark 4, for 50–60 minutes.

Meanwhile, prepare the garnish. Lightly brush the apple rings with oil and grill them until they are light golden-brown on both sides. Remove from the heat and drain on kitchen paper.

Uncover the casserole at the end of the cooking time and garnish with the grilled apple rings and parsley. Serve immediately.

COOK'S NOTES Change the herbs used in this recipe if you prefer. Tarragon, mint, chervil and coriander will all make a good herb crust, too.

Preparation time:
10 minutes

Cooking time:
30–40 minutes

Oven temperature:
190°C (375°F)
Gas Mark 5

Serves: **4**

500 g (1 lb) potatoes, very thinly sliced
2 lemons, sliced
75 g (3 oz) butter
4 red snapper, each about 175 g (6 oz),
filleted
175 g (6 oz) pitted black and green olives
olive oil, for sprinkling
salt and pepper
dill sprigs, to garnish

Arrange the sliced potatoes and lemons in a layer at the bottom of a large, shallow, greased baking dish or roasting tin and dot generously with butter.

Place the fish on top of the potatoes. Season to taste and scatter the olives over the snapper. Sprinkle the fish generously with olive oil and bake in a preheated oven, 190°C (375°F), Gas Mark 5, for about 30–40 minutes, depending on the size of the fish, or until the flesh flakes easily and is tender. Serve immediately, garnished with sprigs of dill.

Preparation time:
5 minutes

Cooking time:
45–50 minutes

Serves: **4**

2 large fennel bulbs
6 tablespoons olive oil
8 tablespoons water
2 sea bass, each about 500 g (1 lb),
filleted
salt and pepper
carrot matchsticks, to garnish

Cut the fennel bulbs lengthways into 1 cm (½ inch) slices. Pour the oil into a wok or large frying pan, add the fennel and water and bring to the boil. Cover and simmer for 30 minutes or until the fennel is very tender, stirring occasionally.

Remove the lid, season the fennel to taste and boil until all the water has evaporated and the fennel is golden-brown. Transfer to a warmed plate and keep hot.

Season the fish, add to the wok or frying pan and baste with the hot oil. Cover and cook for 7–8 minutes. Turn the fish over, baste again and cook for a further 5–6 minutes.

Arrange the fennel on a warmed serving dish, place the fish on the fennel and pour the cooking juices around and over the fish. Serve immediately, garnished with carrot matchsticks.

COOK'S NOTES Ask your fishmonger to fillet the sea bass for you to save time. If you can't get whole sea bass, buy 4 fillets instead, about 175 g (6 oz) each.

145 Seared skate with capers

Preparation time:
5 minutes

Cooking time:
6–8 minutes

Serves: **4**

2 skate wings, each about 300 g (10 oz)
1 teaspoon olive oil
2 tablespoons capers, or caperberries
  with their stalks, halved lengthways
1 tablespoon grated lemon rind
2 tablespoons lemon juice
salt and pepper
lemon wedges, to garnish
steamed vegetable ribbons, to serve

Cut the skate wings in half and pat them dry on kitchen paper. Brush each side with a little oil. Heat a griddle pan and sear the skate wings for 3 minutes on each side. If the wings are thick cook them for a little longer.

Toss the capers or caperberries on top with the lemon rind and juice and cook for a few more seconds. Season to taste and serve garnished with lemon wedges. Serve with steamed ribbons of vegetables.

146 Fresh sardines with pine nuts and anchovies

Preparation time:
30–35 minutes

Cooking time:
40–50 minutes

Oven temperature:
180°C (350°F)
Gas Mark 4

Serves: **4**

75–100 ml (3–3½ fl oz) olive oil
250 g (8 oz) fresh white breadcrumbs
40 g (1½ oz) sultanas, soaked in hot water
  and drained
40 g (1½ oz) pine nuts
1 tablespoon chopped parsley
40 g (1½ oz) canned anchovies, drained
  and chopped
pinch of nutmeg
750 g (1½ lb) sardines, heads and
  backbones removed
about 12 bay leaves
4 tablespoons lemon juice
salt and pepper
lemon wedges, to garnish

Heat 4–5 tablespoons of oil in a frying pan and fry half the breadcrumbs over moderate heat, turning them frequently with a metal spatula until they are a light golden-brown.

Remove from the heat and add the sultanas, pine nuts, parsley, anchovies and nutmeg. Season to taste.

Place a little of the mixture inside each sardine and press the sides together to close. Arrange rows of sardines in a single layer in a large, oiled oven-to-table dish. Place half a bay leaf between each sardine.

Sprinkle the remaining breadcrumbs and the remaining oil over the top and bake in a preheated oven, 180°C (350°F), Gas Mark 4, for 30 minutes. Sprinkle the lemon juice over the top just before serving. Serve hot, garnished with lemon wedges.

COOK'S NOTES If fresh sardines are not available, use sprats or small pilchards instead.

Preparation time: **10 minutes**	**8 skinless plaice fillets**
	1 small onion or shallot, finely chopped
	3 tomatoes, thinly sliced
Cooking time: **20–25 minutes**	**40 g (1½ oz) pepperoni sausage, thinly sliced**
	2 tablespoons chopped flat leaf parsley
Serves: **4**	**1 tablespoon olive oil**
	25 g (1 oz) breadcrumbs
	25 g (1 oz) Parmesan, freshly grated
	salt and pepper
	flat leaf parsley sprigs, to garnish
	lime or lemon wedges, to serve

Lay 4 plaice fillets in a lightly buttered, shallow ovenproof dish. Season lightly and scatter over the onion, then the tomato and pepperoni slices. Sprinkle with parsley and cover with the remaining plaice fillets.

Heat the olive oil in a small frying pan and fry the breadcrumbs until pale golden.

Scatter the breadcrumbs and cheese over the fish. Bake in a preheated oven, 180°C (350°F), Gas Mark 4, for 20–25 minutes or until the fish is cooked through.

Serve the fish garnished with parsley and accompanied by lime or lemon wedges.

Preparation time: **10 minutes**	**750 g (1½ lb) cod or haddock fillets, or a mixture of white fish**
	about 300 ml (1 pint) milk, or milk and water
Cooking time: **15 minutes**	**1 bay leaf**
	½ onion, sliced
Serves: **6**	**6 peppercorns**
	25 g (1 oz) butter or margarine
	3 tablespoons flour
	2 tablespoons chopped parsley or dill
	4 tomatoes, skinned and sliced
	1 kg (2 lb) potatoes
	150 ml (¼ pint) hot milk
	salt and white pepper

Put the fish in a large pan with enough milk or milk and water to cover and with the bay leaf, onion and peppercorns. Simmer gently until the fish is cooked. Strain off the fish liquor into a measuring jug and make it up to 450 ml (¾ pint) with more milk or milk and water if necessary.

Melt the butter or margarine and stir in the flour. Cook over a gentle heat for 1 minute, then stir in the fish liquor. Bring to the boil, stirring, until the sauce is smooth and thick. Season to taste and stir in the chopped parsley or dill. Pour a little sauce into a greased ovenproof dish and lay the fish on top of it. Top with the tomato slices and cover with the remaining sauce.

Meanwhile, boil the potatoes and beat to a purée with the hot milk. Season to taste and pile on top of the fish mixture. Brown under the grill for a few minutes before serving.

COOK'S NOTES If you prefer, use four cod or haddock steaks and simply top them with the stuffing mixture, then add the breadcrumbs and cheese. To test if fish is cooked, pierce the thickest part with the tip of a sharp knife. It should flake easily and be white rather than opaque.

7 Meat Dishes

149 Lasagne

Preparation time: **30 minutes**	**200 g (7 oz) pre-cooked lasagne sheets** **salt and pepper**
Cooking time: **about 1 hour**	MEAT SAUCE: **2 aubergines, peeled and diced** **2 red onions, chopped**
Oven temperature: **180°C (350°F)** **Gas Mark 4**	**2 garlic cloves, crushed** **300 ml (½ pint) Vegetable Stock (see** **introduction)** **4 tablespoons red wine**
Serves: **8**	**500 g (1 lb) lean minced beef** **2 x 400 g (13 oz) cans chopped tomatoes**

CHEESE SAUCE:
3 egg whites
250 g (8 oz) ricotta
175 ml (6 fl oz) milk, or milk and water
6 tablespoons freshly grated Parmesan

First make the meat sauce. Place the aubergines, onions, garlic, stock and wine in a large nonstick saucepan. Cover and simmer briskly for 5 minutes.

Uncover and cook for a further 5 minutes or until the aubergine is tender and the liquid is absorbed, adding a little more stock if necessary. Remove from the heat, allow to cool slightly, then purée in a food processor or blender. Alternatively, push through a coarse sieve.

Meanwhile, brown the mince in a nonstick frying pan. Drain off any fat. Add the aubergine mixture, tomatoes and season to taste. Simmer briskly, uncovered, for about 10 minutes until thickened.

To make the cheese sauce, beat the egg whites with the ricotta. Beat in the milk and 4 tablespoons of Parmesan. Season to taste with pepper.

Alternate layers of meat sauce, lasagne and cheese sauce in an ovenproof dish, starting with meat sauce and finishing with cheese sauce. Sprinkle with the remaining Parmesan. Bake in a preheated oven, 180°C (350°F), Gas Mark 4, for 30–40 minutes until browned.

150 Chilli con carne

Preparation time: **5 minutes**	**2 tablespoons oil** **3 onions, chopped** **1 red pepper, cored, deseeded and diced**
Cooking time: **1–1½ hours**	**1 green pepper, cored, deseeded and** **diced** **2 garlic cloves, crushed**
Serves: **4**	**500 g (1 lb) lean minced beef** **450 ml (¾ pint) Beef Stock (see** **introduction)** **¼–1 teaspoon chilli powder** **475 g (15 oz) canned kidney beans,** **drained** **425 g (14 oz) can chopped tomatoes** **½ teaspoon ground cumin** **salt and pepper** **parsley, to garnish**

TO SERVE:
soft tortillas
soured cream
pickled green chillies
grated Cheddar (optional)

Heat the oil in a large saucepan or flameproof casserole. Add the onions, peppers and garlic and cook gently until soft. Add the meat and fry until just coloured. Blend in the stock and add the chilli powder, beans, tomatoes and cumin. Season to taste.

Bring to the boil, then cover, reduce the heat and simmer gently for 50–60 minutes, stirring occasionally.

Serve the chilli con carne wrapped in soft tortillas, garnished with parsley and accompanied by the soured cream, green chillies and grated cheese, if liked.

151 Green peppercorn steak

Preparation time:
5 minutes

Cooking time:
6–8 minutes

Serves: 4

**4 lean fillet steaks, each about
175 g (6 oz)**
**1 tablespoon green peppercorns in brine,
drained**
2 tablespoons light soy sauce
1 teaspoon balsamic vinegar
8 cherry tomatoes, halved
thyme sprigs, to garnish

Preheat a griddle pan until it is very hot. Cook the steaks for
2–3 minutes on each side. Remove them from the pan and keep hot.

Add the peppercorns, soy sauce, balsamic vinegar and cherry tomatoes
to the griddle pan. Allow the liquids to sizzle for 2 minutes or until the
tomatoes are soft. Spoon the sauce over the steaks and serve
immediately, garnished with sprigs of thyme.

COOK'S NOTES Do not season the steaks with salt before cooking
or you will draw the moisture out of the meat on to the surface, causing
the steaks to boil in their own juices rather than char on the hot griddle.

152 Beef bourguignon

Preparation time:
30 minutes, plus
marinating

Cooking time:
2¾ hours

Serves: 4–6

1 large onion, thinly sliced
6 parsley sprigs
6 thyme sprigs
1 bay leaf, crumbled
**1 kg (2 lb) chuck steak or top rump, cut
into 2.5 cm (1 inch) cubes**
2 tablespoons brandy
400 ml (14 fl oz) red wine
2 tablespoons olive oil
50 g (2 oz) butter
150 g (5 oz) lean bacon, coarsely chopped
24 small pickling onions
500 g (1 lb) button mushrooms, halved
25 g (1 oz) plain flour
**300 ml (½ pint) Beef Stock (see
introduction)**
1 garlic clove, crushed
1 bouquet garni
salt and pepper

Put a few onion slices in a deep bowl with a little parsley, thyme and
some crumbled bay leaf. Place a few pieces of beef on top and
continue layering in this way until all the onion, beef and herbs are
used. Mix the brandy with the wine and oil and pour over the beef.
Cover and leave to marinate for at least 4 hours.

Melt the butter in a flameproof casserole, add the bacon and fry until
golden-brown. Add the small onions and fry until golden on all sides.
Add the mushrooms and fry, stirring, for 1 minute. Drain and set aside.

Remove the beef from the marinade. Strain the marinade and set aside.
Add the beef to the casserole and fry until browned on all sides.
Sprinkle in the flour and cook, stirring, for 1 minute. Gradually stir in the
strained marinade then the stock, garlic and bouquet garni. Season,
cover and simmer gently for 2 hours.

Add the bacon, onions and mushrooms to the casserole, cover and
simmer for 30 minutes. Serve immediately.

153 Beef with colcannon

Preparation time:
25 minutes

Cooking time:
about 1 hour

Serves: 4

1 kg (2 lb) lean casserole steak
2 tablespoons plain flour
2 tablespoons vegetable oil
2 onions, chopped
750 ml (1¼ pints) Beef Stock (see introduction)
150 ml (¼ pint) port (or additional stock)
3 bay leaves
4 pickled walnuts, quartered

COLCANNON:
1 kg (2 lb) floury potatoes, peeled and cut into chunks
500 g (1 lb) Savoy cabbage or spring greens, roughly shredded
25 g (1 oz) butter
1 onion, chopped
4 tablespoons milk
salt and pepper

Cut the beef into chunks, discarding any excess fat. Season the flour with salt and pepper and use it to coat the meat. Heat the oil in a large saucepan, add half the beef and fry quickly until browned. Remove with a slotted spoon and fry the remainder.

Return all the beef to the pan with the onions and fry for 2 minutes. Add the stock, the port (if using) and the bay leaves. Bring just to the boil, then lower the heat, cover the pan and simmer very gently for 1 hour or until the beef is tender. Stir in the walnuts before serving.

Meanwhile, make the colcannon. Cook the potatoes in a large pan of lightly salted boiling water for about 20 minutes or until tender. Add the cabbage to the pan and cook for a further 5 minutes. In the meantime, melt the butter in a small pan, add the onion and fry for 5 minutes.

Drain the potato and cabbage thoroughly and return to the saucepan. Add the onion and milk, season to taste and mash well. Fluff up the surface with a fork and serve with the beef.

154 Stir-fried beef

Preparation time:
20–30 minutes

Cooking time:
9–12 minutes

Serves: 2–3

1 tablespoon Sichuan pepper
3 tablespoons vegetable oil
500 g (1 lb) rump or fillet steak, cut into thin strips across the grain
2 fresh green chillies, deseeded and finely chopped
1 onion, finely sliced
1 red pepper, cored, deseeded and sliced
250 g (8 oz) baby sweetcorn

SAUCE:
3 tablespoons soy sauce
2 tablespoons sake or dry sherry
1 tablespoon dark soft brown sugar
1 teaspoon five-spice powder

Heat a wok or large frying pan until it is hot, add the pepper and dry-fry over a gentle heat for 1–2 minutes. Remove from the pan, crush in a mortar and set aside. Put all the sauce ingredients in a bowl or jug and stir well to mix. Set aside.

Heat the wok or frying pan again until it is hot. Add 2 tablespoons of the oil and heat until hot. Add the beef strips, chillies and crushed peppercorns, increase the heat to high and stir-fry for 3–4 minutes or until the beef is browned on all sides. Remove the wok or pan from the heat and tip the beef and its juices into a bowl. Set aside.

Return the wok or pan to a moderate heat, add the remaining oil and heat until hot. Add the onion and red pepper and stir-fry for 2–3 minutes or until slightly softened. Add the baby sweetcorn and stir-fry for 1–2 minutes or until hot.

Return the beef and its juices to the wok, pour in the sauce and increase the heat to high. Toss for 2–3 minutes or until all the ingredients are combined and piping hot. Serve immediately.

Preparation time: **about 15 minutes, plus marinating**	**1 piece of rump steak, about 375 g (12 oz)** **3 tablespoons vegetable oil** **4 shallots, cut lengthways into chunks** **200 ml (7 fl oz) water**
Cooking time: **15 minutes**	**2 tablespoons soy sauce** **2 tablespoons sake or dry sherry** **1 green chilli, deseeded and chopped**
Serves: **2–3**	**1–2 teaspoons sugar** **3 tangerines, peeled and segmented** **salt and pepper** **1 bunch of coriander, chopped, to garnish**

MARINADE:
grated rind of 1 orange
2 tablespoons soy sauce
1 tablespoon rice wine vinegar
1 tablespoon cornflour
1 teaspoon sugar

Slice the beef into thin strips against the grain. Put the strips in a ceramic dish. Whisk together all the marinade ingredients, pour over the beef and stir to coat thoroughly. Set aside for about 30 minutes.

Preheat a wok. Add 1 tablespoon of the oil, swirl it around the wok, add half the beef and stir-fry over a high heat for 3 minutes. Transfer the beef to a plate using a slotted spoon. Add another tablespoon of oil and stir-fry the remaining beef in the same way. Transfer to the plate.

Heat the remaining oil in the wok, then add the shallots, water, soy sauce, sake or sherry. Sprinkle in the chilli and sugar and season to taste. Bring to the boil, stirring constantly, then stir-fry for about 5 minutes or until the liquid has reduced.

Return the beef to the pan and toss vigorously for 1–2 minutes until all the ingredients are combined and coated with sauce. Add about two-thirds of the tangerine segments and toss quickly to mix. Serve hot, garnished with the remaining tangerine segments and the coriander.

Preparation time: **30 minutes**	**2 tablespoons vegetable oil** **750 g (1½ lb) pie veal, trimmed** **seasoned flour, to dust**
Cooking time: **1½–2 hours**	**150 ml (¼ pint) dry white wine** **1 Spanish onion, finely chopped** **750 g (1½ lb) tomatoes, peeled and**
Serves: **6**	**roughly chopped** **1 teaspoon chopped lemon thyme** **½ teaspoon dried oregano** **150 ml (¼ pint) Chicken Stock (see** **introduction)** **grated rind of 1 lemon** **2 garlic cloves, crushed (optional)** **2 tablespoons chopped parsley** **salt and pepper**

Heat the oil in a large flameproof casserole. Cook the veal, lightly dusted with seasoned flour, until golden.

Add the wine, onion, tomatoes, herbs, stock and seasoning. Bring to a simmering point, cover and cook gently for 1½–2 hours. Take off the lid after the first hour if the sauce needs reducing.

Mix the lemon rind with the garlic and parsley. Sprinkle over the casserole just before serving.

COOK'S NOTES Spanish onions are larger and milder than many other varieties, and will impart a delicate flavour to the dish.

Preparation time:	**3–4 tablespoons olive oil**
5 minutes	**25 g (1 oz) butter**
	500 g (1 lb) onions, sliced
Cooking time:	**1 tablespoon chopped parsley, plus extra**
10–15 minutes	**to garnish**
	500 g (1 lb) calves' liver, thinly sliced
Serves: **4**	**4 tablespoons Beef Stock (see**
	introduction)
	salt and pepper

TO SERVE:

mashed potatoes
sautéed mushrooms

Heat the oil and butter in a frying pan, add the onions and parsley and cook gently for 2–3 minutes.

Add the liver, increase the heat and stir in the stock. Cook the liver for 5 minutes, then remove from the heat and season to taste.

Serve immediately with mashed potatoes, topped with sautéed mushrooms and garnished with parsley.

Preparation time:	**4 lean venison cutlets**
20 minutes, plus	**150 ml (¼ pint) brown ale**
marinating	**3 teaspoons olive oil**
	1 garlic clove, crushed
Cooking time:	**2 dried bay leaves, crumbled**
10–12 minutes	**1 teaspoon soft light brown sugar**
	pepper
Serves: **4**	

Trim any visible fat from the venison cutlets and place them in a single layer in a shallow dish. Pour over the brown ale and olive oil.

Add the garlic and bay leaves, pepper and sugar, but do not add salt. Cover the dish and place it in the refrigerator to marinate for at least 4 hours, or overnight.

Lift the venison out of the marinade, reserving the liquid. Place the cutlets on a hot barbecue or preheated griddle pan and cook them for 10–12 minutes, turning once. They should be browned on the outside but slightly pink on the inside. Spoon over the marinade while cooking to prevent the meat from drying.

COOK'S NOTES This dish freezes particularly well. Freeze the venison in the marinade in a freezer-proof container. It will keep for up to a month. Defrost in a refrigerator overnight.

Preparation time:	1–2 tablespoons oil
25 minutes	1 onion, finely chopped
	750 g–1 kg (1½–2 lb) lean, boneless
Cooking time:	venison, cut into 2.5 cm (1 inch) cubes
1½–2 hours	25 g (1 oz) plain flour
	300 ml (½ pint) Guinness or stout
Serves: 4–6	750 ml (1¼ pints) Chicken Stock or Beef
	Stock (see introduction) or water
	1 bay leaf
	1 marjoram sprig
	12–18 pickling onions, peeled
	125–175 g (4–6 oz) celery, cut into 2.5 cm
	(1 inch) lengths
	2 tablespoons finely chopped parsley
	salt and pepper
	mashed potatoes or champ, to serve

Heat half the oil in a large frying pan and fry the onion until it is soft and beginning to brown. Transfer the onion to a large flameproof casserole dish.

Heat the remaining oil in the pan and fry the meat, a little at a time, until it is brown. Add to the onion. Stir in the flour and add the Guinness or stout and the stock, together with the bay leaf and marjoram. Season to taste.

Bring to the boil, then lower the heat and simmer gently for 1–1½ hours, until the meat is almost tender. Add the onions and celery 15–30 minutes before the end of cooking time.

To serve, taste the stew and adjust the seasoning if necessary. Stir in the finely chopped parsley and serve with mashed potatoes or champ.

COOK'S NOTES This stew can also be cooked in an oven instead of on the stove top. Place the casserole dish in a preheated oven, 160°C (325°F), Gas Mark 3, for 1½–2 hours.

Preparation time:	8 lamb chops or lamb leg steaks, about
5 minutes, plus	2.5 cm (1 inch) thick
marinating	175 ml (6 fl oz) red wine
	1–2 tablespoons olive oil
Cooking time:	5 tablespoons finely chopped mint
15–20 minutes	salt and pepper
	mixed leaf salad, to serve
Serves: 4	

TO GARNISH:
mint or parsley sprigs
tomato wedges

Put the lamb chops or steaks in a shallow, ceramic dish. Mix together the wine, oil and chopped mint, then pour the mixture over the meat, turning to coat thoroughly. Cover and set aside to marinate in a cool place for 1 hour, turning the lamb after about 30 minutes.

Remove the lamb from the marinade and cook on a preheated, greased barbecue grill or under a conventional grill for 7–10 minutes on each side, depending on whether the meat is to be rare or well done. Baste with any leftover marinade before turning.

Sprinkle the lamb with salt and pepper to taste and serve very hot, with a leafy salad, garnished with the mint or parsley and tomato wedges.

161 Braised lamb

162 Mountain lamb

Preparation time:	**3 tablespoons olive oil**
20 minutes	**2 celery sticks, chopped**
	375 g (12 oz) pickling onions
Cooking time:	**1 kg (2 lb) boned leg or shoulder of lamb,**
1½ hours	**cut into serving pieces**
	2 rosemary sprigs, chopped, plus extra
Serves: **4**	**to garnish**
	2 bay leaves
	450 ml (¾ pint) Chicken Stock (see
	introduction)
	salt and pepper

Heat the oil in a flameproof casserole, add the celery and onions and fry gently for 5 minutes.

Add the meat, the rosemary and the bay leaves. Season to taste. Fry over moderate heat until the meat is browned on all sides.

Stir in the stock and just enough water to cover the meat. Cover the casserole and simmer for 1 hour or until the meat is tender. Discard the herbs before serving. Serve hot, garnished with rosemary.

Preparation time:	**3 tablespoons olive oil**
10 minutes	**1 kg (2 lb) boned shoulder or leg of lamb,**
	cut into serving pieces
Cooking time:	**500 g (1 lb) mushrooms, sliced**
1¼ hours	**125 ml (4 fl oz) dry white wine**
	salt and pepper
Oven temperature:	
190°C (375°F)	TO SERVE:
Gas Mark 5	**steamed spinach**
	polenta slices
Serves: **4**	

Heat the oil in a flameproof casserole, add the meat and fry over moderate heat until browned on all sides.

Add the mushrooms, wine and enough water to just cover the meat. Season to taste.

Cover and cook in a preheated oven, 190°C (375°F), Gas Mark 5, for 1 hour or until the meat is tender, stirring occasionally.

Serve hot, with steamed spinach and slices of polenta.

COOK'S NOTES This is a good way to use an economical joint like shoulder of lamb. Buy the leanest piece you can find, however, as it can be rather fatty. If necessary, ask your butcher to remove the bone for you.

163 Italian lamb with rosemary oil

164 Sardinian lamb

Preparation time:	2 lamb fillets, trimmed of fat, about
20 minutes	750 g (1½ lb) in total
	4 garlic cloves, finely sliced
Cooking time:	**handful of small rosemary sprigs**
20–40 minutes	**2 red onions, quartered**
	1 tablespoon chopped rosemary
Serves: **4**	**4 tablespoons olive oil**
	salt and pepper

TO SERVE:
fresh pasta
Parmesan shavings

Make small incisions with a sharp knife all over the lamb fillets and insert the garlic slivers and rosemary sprigs. Heat a griddle pan until hot, put on the fillets and cook, turning the lamb occasionally, until it is charred all over. This will take about 20 minutes for rare meat or 30–40 minutes for well done meat. Add the onions for the last 10 minutes and char on the outside.

Place the chopped rosemary and oil in a mortar and crush with a pestle to release the flavours. Season to taste. Allow the lamb to rest for 5 minutes before carving into slices. Spoon the rosemary oil over the top and serve immediately with the griddled onions. Serve with fresh pasta, lightly tossed in olive oil, and Parmesan shavings.

Preparation time:	5 tablespoons olive oil
20 minutes	**1 kg (2 lb) boned leg of lamb, cut into**
	serving pieces
Cooking time:	**1 onion, chopped**
1–1½ hours	**400 g (14 oz) tomatoes, skinned and**
	mashed
Serves: **4**	**750 g (1½ lb) fennel, quartered**
	salt and pepper

Heat the oil in a flameproof casserole, add the meat and fry over moderate heat until lightly browned on all sides.

Stir in the onion and fry for a further 5 minutes. Add the tomatoes and season to taste.

Reduce the heat, cover and simmer for 40 minutes, adding a little water if the casserole becomes too dry during cooking.

Meanwhile, cook the fennel in boiling salted water for 20 minutes. Drain and reserve 200 ml (7 fl oz) of the cooking liquid.

Add the fennel and the reserved cooking liquid to the casserole, and continue cooking for about 20 minutes until the meat is tender. The casserole should be fairly dry. Serve hot, sprinkled with black pepper.

COOK'S NOTES Two types of lamb fillets are suitable for this dish: the more expensive and leaner loin fillets, or the more fatty but less expensive neck fillets.

Preparation time:
30 minutes, plus marinating

Cooking time:
10–15 minutes

Serves: **4**

200 g (7 oz) leg of lamb, cut into fine strips
4 small tomatoes, halved
125 g (4 oz) button mushrooms
1 green pepper, cored, deseeded and cut into 2.5 cm (1 inch) squares
8 bay leaves (optional)

MARINADE:
150 ml (¼ pint) natural yogurt
juice of 1 lemon
1 teaspoon salt
2 teaspoons pepper
1 small onion, finely chopped

Preparation time:
20 minutes

Cooking time:
12 minutes

Serves: **4**

750 g (1½ lb) minced lamb
1 bunch of parsley, chopped
1 onion, chopped
1 garlic clove, crushed
dash of tabasco
1 egg, beaten
4 small naan breads
1 red onion, sliced
3 tomatoes, halved and finely sliced
1 large bunch of mint, chopped
2 tablespoons olive oil
2 tablespoons lemon juice
salt and pepper

Trim all visible fat from the meat.

Mix together all the marinade ingredients in a bowl. Place the meat in the marinade and leave for about 24 hours, turning occasionally.

Reserve the marinade and thread the strips of meat on to four long or eight short skewers, alternating with the tomatoes, mushrooms, pepper and the bay leaves, if using.

Cook under a hot grill, turning once, for 10–15 minutes. Brush the vegetables with the marinade once or twice during cooking so they do not dry out. Serve with boiled rice and salad.

Mix together the lamb, parsley, onion, garlic, tabasco and egg. Season to taste and shape the mixture into eight sausages that will fit into the naan breads.

Heat a griddle pan until hot. Place the lamb sausages on the griddle and cook for 6–9 minutes. Take care when turning the sausages; it is important to get a good crust on the outside of the sausages so that they don't break when turned.

Mix together the onion, tomatoes, mint, olive oil, lemon juice and seasoning. Open the naan breads carefully, making a pocket in which to place the filling.

Place the naan breads under a medium grill and cook on each side until lightly browned. Fill with the salad and add the sausages. Serve immediately.

COOK'S NOTES This recipe is equally delicious made with minced pork, beef or chicken.

167 Lamb and courgette koftas

168 Pork with rosemary and fennel

Preparation time:	**2 courgettes, finely grated**
20 minutes	**2 tablespoons sesame seeds**
	250 g (8 oz) minced lamb
Cooking time:	**2 spring onions, finely chopped**
5 minutes per batch	**1 garlic clove, crushed**
	1 tablespoon chopped mint
Serves: **4**	**½ teaspoon ground mixed spice**
	2 tablespoons dried breadcrumbs
	1 egg, lightly beaten
	vegetable oil, for shallow-frying
	salt and pepper
	lemon wedges, to garnish

Place the finely grated courgettes in a sieve and press down to extract as much liquid as possible. Place the courgettes in a bowl.

Dry-fry the sesame seeds in a large frying pan for 1–2 minutes or until they are golden and release their aroma. Add them to the courgettes, together with the lamb and all the remaining ingredients, except the oil and lemon. Season liberally with salt and pepper.

Form the mixture into 20 small balls and shallow-fry in batches for 5 minutes, turning frequently until evenly browned. Keep the koftas warm in a hot oven while you are cooking the rest. Serve hot, garnished with lemon wedges.

Preparation time:	**750 g (1½ lb) pork fillet, trimmed of any fat**
15 minutes	**handful of rosemary sprigs, broken into small pieces**
Cooking time:	**3 garlic cloves, sliced lengthways**
30 minutes	**4 tablespoons olive oil**
	2 fennel bulbs
Oven temperature:	**300 ml (½ pint) white wine**
230°C (450°F)	**150 g (5 oz) mascarpone**
Gas Mark 8	**salt and pepper**
Serves: **2**	

Pierce the pork with a sharp knife blade and insert small sprigs of rosemary and slices of garlic evenly all over the fillet.

Heat 2 tablespoons of olive oil in a frying pan, add the pork fillet and fry for 5 minutes or until browned.

Trim the fennel, cut it into wedges and remove the solid central core. Lightly oil a roasting pan, place the trimmed fennel in it and drizzle over the remaining olive oil. Place the pork on top and season. Place in a preheated oven, 230°C (450°F), Gas Mark 8, and roast for 25 minutes.

Add the wine to the frying pan in which the pork was fried and simmer, until reduced by half. Add the mascarpone, season to taste and stir to mix thoroughly.

Serve the pork in slices with the wedges of fennel. Pour the sauce into the roasting pan and simmer over a low heat on top of the stove until it has slightly thickened. Stir well and spoon over the pork and fennel.

COOK'S NOTES Even if you buy ready-minced lamb, it is worth working it in a food processor or mincer before making the koftas to make sure that it is really finely minced. If you buy the lamb in one piece, process it twice in the food processor or mincer.

Preparation time:	2 pork tenderloins, each 375 g (12 oz),
15 minutes	**trimmed**
	2 tablespoons olive oil
Cooking time:	**75 g (3 oz) butter, diced**
30 minutes	**2 shallots, finely chopped**
	1 small garlic clove, crushed
Oven temperature:	**2 teaspoons chopped sage**
190°C (375°F)	**125 ml (4 fl oz) marsala**
Gas Mark 5	**150 ml (¼ pint) Chicken Stock (see**
	introduction)
Serves: **4**	**salt and pepper**
	sage leaves, deep-fried in a little olive
	oil until crisp, to garnish (optional)
	buttered spinach or greens, to serve

Season the pork well with salt and pepper. Heat the oil in a large, ovenproof frying pan, add the meat and fry for about 5 minutes, until well browned on all sides. Transfer to a preheated oven, 190°C (375°F), Gas Mark 5, and roast for about 20 minutes or until the pork is cooked through. To test, push a skewer into the centre of the meat; the juices should run clear. Remove the pork from the pan and wrap it in foil to rest while you make the sauce.

Meanwhile, add 25 g (1 oz) of the butter to the pan and gently fry the shallots, garlic and sage for 5 minutes or until softened.

Deglaze the pan with the marsala by boiling rapidly for 1–2 minutes or until slightly reduced, then add the stock and simmer for 5 minutes. Reduce the heat and gradually whisk in the remaining butter, a little at a time, until the sauce is thickened and glossy.

Cut the pork into slices, pour over the sauce and garnish with fried sage leaves, if using. Serve with buttered spinach or greens

.

Preparation time:	1.75 kg (3½ lb) pork loin joint
15 minutes	**50 g (2 oz) bulgar wheat**
	300 ml (½ pint) boiling water
Cooking time:	**1 small onion, finely chopped**
about 2½ hours	**2 celery sticks, finely chopped**
	50 g (2 oz) mushrooms, finely chopped
Oven temperature:	**1 tablespoon chopped sage**
160°C (325°F)	**2 tablespoons natural yogurt**
Gas Mark 3	**salt and pepper**
	celery leaves, to garnish
Serves: **6**	

Remove the skin and most of the fat from the pork, leaving only a thin layer, then score the surface into a diamond pattern. Turn the meat over and, using a sharp knife, remove the bones.

Place the bulgar wheat in a saucepan, pour over the water and bring back to the boil. Cover and simmer for 10–15 minutes or until the liquid has been absorbed. Stir in the onion, celery, mushrooms, sage and yogurt. Season to taste.

Spread the stuffing over the pork, roll it up and tie with fine cotton string. Place the pork on a rack in a roasting tin and sprinkle with pepper. Roast in a preheated oven, 160°C (325°F), Gas Mark 3, basting occasionally with the juices in the tin, for about 2 hours or until the juices run clear. Garnish with celery leaves. Skim the juices and serve as a gravy.

COOK'S NOTES Bulgar wheat, or cracked wheat, is wheat that has been hulled and steamed, then cracked and dried, resulting in small grains.

Preparation time:	**8 speciality sausages**
10 minutes	**2 onions, cut into wedges, roots left intact**
Cooking time:	
25 minutes	MUSTARD MASH:
	1 kg (2 lb) potatoes, quartered but left
Serves: **4**	**unpeeled**
	75 g (3 oz) butter
	1 tablespoon wholegrain mustard
	3 teaspoons English mustard
	1 garlic clove, crushed
	1 large bunch of parsley, chopped
	dash of olive oil
	salt and pepper

Place the potatoes in a saucepan of cold water, bring to the boil and simmer for 15 minutes.

Heat a griddle pan until hot. Place the sausages on the griddle and cook for 10 minutes, turning to get an even colour. Add the onion wedges and cook for 6–7 minutes with the sausages.

When the potatoes are cooked, drain well and return to the pan, place over a low heat and allow any excess water to evaporate but take care that the potatoes do not colour. Remove from the heat and peel. Mash them thoroughly, add the butter, mustards and garlic and season to taste. Taste the potato and add more mustard if liked. Finally, add the parsley and a dash of olive oil and stir.

Serve the mash and sausages together with the griddled onion wedges.

Preparation time:	**1 onion, finely chopped**
about 10 minutes	**1 teaspoon olive oil**
	4 rabbit joints, each about 200 g (7 oz)
Cooking time:	**300 ml (½ pint) Chicken Stock (see**
about 55 minutes	**introduction)**
	200 ml (7 fl oz) dry white wine
Serves: **4**	**2 teaspoons coarse-grain mustard**
	1 tablespoon chopped rosemary
	3 tablespoons fromage frais
	1 egg yolk
	salt and pepper
	rosemary sprigs, to garnish

Fry the onion gently in the olive oil for 3 minutes. Add the rabbit joints and brown evenly on all sides.

Add the chicken stock, white wine, mustard and rosemary. Season to taste. Cover and simmer for 45 minutes or until the rabbit is just tender. Remove the rabbit joints to a serving dish and keep warm.

Boil the cooking liquid rapidly until it is reduced by half. Beat the fromage frais with the egg yolk and whisk into the cooking liquid over a gentle heat, without boiling.

Spoon the sauce over the rabbit and garnish with sprigs of rosemary.

COOK'S NOTES If you are using frozen rabbit, make sure the joints are completely defrosted before cooking. Other mustards can be used, but they will not give the same texture as coarse-grain mustard.

8 Chicken and Poultry Dishes

173 Chicken and mushroom pie

174 Clay-pot baked spring chicken

Preparation time: **40 minutes, plus** **cooling**	**1.5 kg (3 lb) chicken with giblets** **1 bouquet garni** **1 small onion, quartered** **6–8 black peppercorns**
Cooking time: **about 1½ hours**	**25 g (1 oz) butter** **2 leeks, thinly sliced** **125 g (4 oz) button mushrooms, sliced**
Oven temperature: **190°C (375°F)** **Gas Mark 5**	**1 teaspoon plain flour** **125 g (4 oz) full-fat soft cheese** **2 tablespoons chopped parsley**
Serves: **6**	TOPPING: **500 g (1 lb) potatoes, cut into chunks** **250 g (8 oz) carrots, sliced** **25 g (1 oz) butter** **1 egg, beaten** **pinch of ground nutmeg** **salt and pepper**

Put the chicken and giblets into a large saucepan with the bouquet garni, onion, black peppercorns and a little salt. Cover with water, bring to the boil, and skim any fat from the surface. Cover the pan and simmer for about 1 hour or until the chicken is cooked. Remove the chicken and set aside. When it is cool enough to handle, cut the meat from the bones, place it in an ovenproof dish and set aside. Melt the butter in a small pan and fry the leeks and mushrooms over a moderate heat for 3 minutes, stirring. Stir in the flour, then the soft cheese and chopped parsley. Simmer for 3 minutes, then spread the vegetables over the pieces of chicken.

Cook the potatoes and carrots separately in large saucepans of lightly salted boiling water for about 20 minutes or until tender. Drain well then mash them together, using a potato masher or fork, and beat in the butter and egg. Season to taste with nutmeg, salt and pepper. Spread the potato and carrot topping evenly over the chicken and vegetables, then fork it up into peaks. Bake in a preheated oven, 190°C (375°F), Gas Mark 5, for 20–25 minutes or until the topping is browned.

Preparation time: **15 minutes, plus** **standing**	**1.5 kg (3 lb) free-range chicken** **1 lemon, pricked or slashed** **2 rosemary sprigs, plus extra to garnish** **2 red peppers, halved, cored and** **deseeded**
Cooking time: **1 hour 50 minutes**	**2 yellow peppers, halved, cored and** **deseeded**
Oven temperature: **200°C (400°F)** **Gas Mark 6**	**300 ml (½ pint) Chicken Stock (see** **introduction)** **salt and pepper** **lemon wedges, to garnish**
Serves: **4**	

Soak a clay pot for 10 minutes in cold water. Meanwhile, remove the giblets from the chicken, rinse the cavity and pat the chicken dry with kitchen paper.

Push the lemon and rosemary into the cavity. Drain the water from the clay pot, put the chicken in the pot and lay the pepper pieces around. Pour over the chicken stock, season well and cover with the clay pot lid.

Put the pot into a cold oven and then bake at 200°C (400°F), Gas Mark 6, for 1 hour 50 minutes.

Remove the chicken and peppers from the pot and allow the chicken to stand for 10 minutes. Meanwhile, strain off the fat from the cooking juices by letting them drain through the hole in the clay pot. Pour the cooking liquid into a saucepan and boil rapidly for 5 minutes.

Serve the chicken garnished with a wedge of the lemon and fresh rosemary sprigs with the reduced stock and the peppers.

COOK'S NOTES A clay pot is specially designed for cooking meat, keeping it moist and tender in the oven. It will come in two parts: a base and a close-fitting lid to trap the steam.

175 Chicken and courgette bake

176 Pot-roast chicken

Preparation time: **15 minutes**	**750 g (1½ lb) courgettes, sliced diagonally**
	50 g (2 oz) Edam, grated
Cooking time: **20 minutes**	**175 g (6 oz) cooked chicken, skinned and diced**
	75 g (3 oz) cooked ham, diced
Oven temperature: **190°C (375°F) Gas Mark 5**	**3 tomatoes, sliced**
	SAUCE:
Serves: **6**	**25 g (1 oz) butter or margarine**
	25 g (1 oz) plain flour
	300 ml (½ pint) milk
	1 tablespoon sherry (optional)
	salt and pepper

Preparation time: **5 minutes**	**2 tablespoons olive oil**
	15 g (½ oz) unsalted butter
	1 chicken, about 1.75 kg (3½ lb), jointed
Cooking time: **about 1 hour 10 minutes**	**2 garlic cloves, crushed**
	125 ml (4 fl oz) dry white wine
	1 rosemary sprig
	2 tablespoons lemon juice
Serves: **4**	**5–6 fine strips of lemon rind**
	salt and pepper
	TO SERVE:
	steamed carrot and courgette ribbons
	cooked long-grain rice, mixed with chopped herbs

Cook the courgettes in boiling salted water for 4–5 minutes. Drain well on kitchen paper and place in an ovenproof dish.

Sprinkle half the cheese over the courgettes. Arrange the chicken, ham and sliced tomatoes in layers over the top and sprinkle with the remaining cheese.

Next make the sauce. Melt the butter or margarine in a small saucepan over a moderate heat. Stir in the flour and cook for 1 minute. Gradually add the milk, stirring continuously. Bring the sauce to the boil and let it cook for 2–3 minutes. Season to taste and blend in the sherry, if using. Pour the sauce over the meat, courgettes and tomatoes. Place in a preheated oven, 190°C (375°F), Gas Mark 5, for 20 minutes or until golden. Serve hot.

Heat the oil and butter in a heavy flameproof casserole. Add the chicken, skin side down, and fry over a medium heat until lightly browned all over, adding the garlic towards the end.

Stir in the wine, add the rosemary and season to taste. Bring to the boil for 2–3 minutes, then lower the heat, cover tightly and cook over a very low heat, turning the chicken a couple of times, for 45–50 minutes or until the juices run clear.

Remove the chicken and transfer it to a warmed serving plate. Cover it and keep it warm.

Meanwhile, make the sauce. Discard the rosemary and skim off most of the fat from the cooking juices. Stir in the lemon juice to dislodge the sediment. Add the strips of lemon rind and bring to the boil over a high heat, stirring constantly. Pour the sauce over the chicken and serve immediately with carrot and courgette ribbons and rice mixed with chopped herbs.

COOK'S NOTES This is a good dish for a low-fat diet, and can be made with low-fat spread instead of butter or margarine, and skimmed milk. Edam cheese is already lower in fat than other hard cheeses.

Preparation time:	**125 g (4 oz) long-grain rice**
30 minutes	**1 chicken, about 1.5 kg (3 lb), with giblets**
	300 ml (½ pint) Chicken Stock (see
Cooking time:	**introduction)**
2 hours 10 minutes	**50 g (2 oz) raisins**
	1 small green pepper, chopped
Oven temperature:	**grated rind of 1 lemon**
180°C (350°F)	**500 g (1 lb) onions, quartered**
Gas Mark 4	**500 g (1 lb) baby carrots**
	500 g (1 lb) small tomatoes, peeled and
Serves: **6**	**quartered**
	¼ teaspoon chopped rosemary
	300 ml (½ pint) dry cider
	lemon juice
	salt and pepper
	boiled potatoes tossed in chopped
	parsley, to serve

Cook the rice in boiling, salted water for 10 minutes or until tender. Drain well. Chop the chicken liver and cook for a few minutes in a little stock. Drain. Mix together the rice, chicken livers, raisins, green pepper, grated lemon rind and seasoning. Stuff the chicken with this mixture.

Grease a casserole dish large enough to hold the chicken comfortably. Place the onions, carrots and tomatoes in the bottom and lay the chicken on top. Sprinkle the chicken with the rosemary and pour over the cider.

Cover the casserole and cook in a preheated oven, 180°C (350°F), Gas Mark 4, for 2 hours until the chicken is tender. Remove the lid for the last 10 minutes to brown the chicken.

Lift out the chicken and place on a warmed serving dish. Remove the vegetables carefully with a slotted spoon and arrange them round the chicken. Strain the juices from the casserole into a small pan and add a squeeze of lemon juice. Reheat and serve separately, in a jug or sauceboat. Serve the chicken with boiled potatoes tossed in chopped parsley.

Preparation time:	**3 tablespoons olive oil**
5 minutes	**1 tablespoon butter**
	4 chicken breasts, skinned
Cooking time:	**175 ml (6 fl oz) dry white wine**
25–30 minutes	**4–6 sage leaves, roughly chopped, plus**
	extra to garnish
Serves: **4**	**3 tablespoons balsamic vinegar**
	salt and pepper

Heat the oil and butter in a large nonstick frying pan until foaming. Add the chicken and cook over a low to moderate heat for 5–7 minutes until golden-brown on both sides, turning once.

Pour the wine over the chicken and sprinkle over the chopped sage. Season to taste. Cover and cook over a low heat for 15 minutes, spooning the sauce over the chicken from time to time and turning the chicken halfway through cooking.

Remove the chicken to warmed plates and keep warm. Add the balsamic vinegar to the pan juices, increase the heat to high and stir until the juices are reduced. Spoon the juices over the chicken, garnish with sage and serve immediately.

COOK'S NOTES Chicken breasts on the bone have the most tender and moist meat, and they are less likely to dry out during cooking. They are available in some good supermarkets. Boneless chicken breasts are easier to obtain, but take care to baste them frequently.

179 Carnival chicken

Preparation time:
15–20 minutes, plus
marinating

Cooking time:
20 minutes

Serves: 4

4 skinless chicken breasts, each about
150 g (5 oz)
flat leaf parsley sprigs, to garnish

MARINADE:
100 ml (3½ fl oz) sweet sherry
1 teaspoon Angostura bitters
1 tablespoon light soy sauce
1 tablespoon chopped fresh root ginger
pinch of ground cumin
pinch of ground coriander
1 teaspoon dried mixed herbs
1 small onion, finely chopped
75 ml (3 fl oz) Chicken Stock (see
introduction)

SWEET POTATO MASH:
2 sweet potatoes
2 tablespoons fromage frais (optional)
salt and pepper

Place the chicken breasts in a ceramic dish. In a bowl mix together all the marinade ingredients. Spoon over the chicken, making sure the pieces are well coated. Cover and leave to marinate in the refrigerator for 4 hours or overnight.

When you are ready to cook, place the chicken on a grill pan and cook under a preheated medium grill for 20 minutes, turning over halfway through cooking.

Meanwhile, make the mash. Boil the sweet potatoes in their skins for 20 minutes or until soft. Drain well and peel. Mash the potato and let it dry off a little, then stir in the fromage frais, if using. Season and serve with the chicken. Garnish the flat leaf parsley.

180 Grilled devilled chicken

Preparation time:
10 minutes, plus
marinating

Cooking time:
30–40 minutes

Serves: 4

625 g (1¼ lb) chicken portions, skinned
1 tablespoon French mustard
1 teaspoon ground ginger
1 teaspoon salt
1 teaspoon pepper
1 teaspoon Worcestershire sauce
½ teaspoon sugar
juice of 1 lemon

Place the chicken portions in a shallow ovenproof dish. Mix together the mustard, ginger, salt, pepper, Worcestershire sauce, sugar and lemon juice. Use the mixture to coat the chicken portions and leave to marinate for several hours, turning occasionally in the marinade.

Place the chicken portions under a preheated grill or on a barbecue, not too close to the coals. Allow 15–20 minutes on each side, although the cooking time may be shorter if you do this on an outside barbecue.

COOK'S NOTES Make sure chicken is thoroughly cooked before serving. To test if it is cooked, pierce through the thickest part with a fine skewer or pointed knife. The juices should run clear. If they are pink, cook for a little longer and test again.

181 Blackened chicken skewers

182 Mandarin chicken

Preparation time:
5 minutes, plus marinating

Cooking time:
20 minutes

Serves: **4**

300 g (10 oz) boneless, skinless chicken breast, diced
1 tablespoon Cajun seasoning mix
2 tablespoons lemon juice
1 teaspoon olive oil
coriander sprigs, to garnish

TO SERVE:
boiled rice
green salad

Place the chicken in a bowl and add the seasoning mix, lemon juice and olive oil. Toss well and leave to marinate for 15 minutes. Meanwhile, soak 8 wooden skewers in warm water.

Drain the skewers and thread the pieces of chicken on to them. Cover the ends of the skewers with foil, place under a preheated medium grill and cook for 20 minutes, turning over halfway through cooking. When the chicken is cooked through, remove from the grill and reserve any juices. Remove the chicken from the skewers and garnish with coriander sprigs. Serve with the juices, boiled rice and a green salad.

Preparation time:
5 minutes, plus marinating

Cooking time:
20 minutes

Serves: **4**

500 g (1 lb) boneless, skinless chicken breast, diced
300 g (10 oz) can mandarin segments in juice, drained (reserve the juice)
grated rind and juice of 1 lemon
4 spring onions, shredded
2 tablespoons Thai seven-spice seasoning
1 tablespoon dark soy sauce

TO SERVE:
cooked noodles
sliced spring onions
sliced red chillies

Place the diced chicken in a bowl with the mandarin juice, lemon rind and juice, spring onions, seven-spice seasoning and soy sauce. Stir to combine and leave to marinate, covered, in a refrigerator for at least 1 hour or overnight.

Before cooking, soak 4 wooden skewers in warm water for 10 minutes, then drain.

Thread the chicken and mandarin segments on to the skewers, packing them tightly together so the fruit does not fall off. Place under a preheated medium grill and cook for 10 minutes. Turn the skewers, baste with any remaining marinade and cook for a further 10 minutes. Serve on a bed of noodles, tossed with spring onions and red chillies.

COOK'S NOTES Cajun seasoning mix is available from specialist West Indian food shops and in many supermarkets.

183 Lemon chicken

Preparation time:	**1 tablespoon olive oil**
15 minutes	**1 small onion, finely sliced**
	4 chicken breasts, each about 75 g (3 oz),
Cooking time:	**skinned and boned**
30–35 minutes	**2 tablespoons chopped parsley**
	300 ml (½ pint) Chicken Stock (see
Serves: **4**	**introduction)**
	1 tablespoon clear honey
	juice of 1 lemon
	2 teaspoons cornflour
	1 tablespoon water
	rind of 1 lemon, cut into matchstick strips
	salt and pepper

Heat the oil in a large frying pan. Add the onion and fry gently for 3–4 minutes. Add the chicken and fry until lightly browned all over.

Add the parsley, stock, honey, and lemon juice and season to taste. Cover the pan and simmer gently for 20 minutes.

Use a slotted spoon to remove the chicken breasts to a warmed serving dish and keep warm.

Blend the cornflour and water to a smooth paste, stir in a little of the hot cooking liquid and then return to the pan. Stir over gentle heat until thickened. Add the strips of lemon rind to the sauce and spoon evenly over the chicken.

COOK'S NOTES Honey is more commonly known for its use in sweet dishes but it also has a place in many meat dishes. It is a popular flavouring in savoury cooking around the world, including North Africa, China and the United States.

184 Chicken with ginger

Preparation time:	**375 g (12 oz) boneless, skinless chicken**
20 minutes, plus	**breast**
marinating	**1 tablespoon dry sherry**
	4 spring onions, chopped
Cooking time:	**2.5 cm (1 inch) fresh root ginger, finely**
4–5 minutes	**chopped**
	3 teaspoons oil
Serves: **4**	**1–2 garlic cloves, finely sliced**
	2 celery sticks, sliced diagonally
	1 small green pepper, cored, deseeded
	and sliced
	2 tablespoons light soy sauce
	juice of ½ lemon
	shredded rind of 2 lemons
	¼ teaspoon chilli powder

TO GARNISH:
lemon wedges
parsley sprigs

Cut the chicken into 8 cm (3 inch) strips. Combine the sherry, spring onions and ginger, add the chicken and toss well to coat. Set aside to marinate for 15 minutes.

Heat the oil in a large, nonstick frying pan or wok. Add the garlic, celery and green pepper and stir-fry for 1 minute. Add the chicken and the marinade and cook for 2 minutes. Stir in the soy sauce, lemon juice and rind and chilli powder and cook for a further 1 minute.

Pile into a warmed serving dish, garnish with lemon wedges and parsley sprigs and serve immediately.

Preparation time:	4 boneless, skinless chicken breasts
10 minutes, plus marinating	**flat leaf parsley, to garnish**
	TANDOORI MARINADE:
Cooking time:	**300 ml (½ pint) natural yogurt**
20 minutes	**1 cm (½ inch) fresh root ginger, finely chopped**
Serves: **4**	**1 garlic clove, crushed**
	2 teaspoons paprika
	1 teaspoon chilli powder
	1 tablespoon tomato purée
	finely grated rind and juice of ½ lemon
	salt and pepper

TO SERVE:
**lime wedges
mixed salad**

Mix all the marinade ingredients together and season to taste with salt and pepper. Pour into a shallow, non-metallic dish. Prick the chicken breasts all over with a fine skewer and place in the marinade, turning to coat well. Cover and set aside to marinate overnight in a cool place, turning the chicken occasionally.

Remove the chicken from the marinade and place under a preheated hot grill. Cook for about 10 minutes on each side, or until the chicken is tender and the juices run clear.

Garnish with parsley sprigs and serve with lime wedges and a mixed salad, if liked.

COOK'S NOTES This chicken is particularly tasty when cooked on a barbecue. Allow the edges to blacken a little to get the full flavour.

Preparation time:	4 boneless chicken breasts, cubed
45 minutes, plus marinating	**juice of 1 lemon**
	1½ teaspoons salt
	2 teaspoons pepper
Cooking time:	**1 onion, quartered**
about 20 minutes	**2 garlic cloves**
	5 cm (2 inches) fresh root ginger, peeled
Serves: **4–6**	**375 g (12 oz) natural yogurt**
	chopped parsley, to garnish

MASALA:
**75 g (3 oz) ghee or butter
1 onion, finely sliced
1 garlic clove, finely sliced
1½ teaspoons turmeric
1½ teaspoons chilli powder
1 teaspoon ground cinnamon
seeds from 20 cardamom pods
1 teaspoon ground coriander
2 teaspoons aniseed**

Place the chicken in a bowl and sprinkle with lemon juice, salt and pepper. Coat the chicken, then cover and set aside. Place the onion, garlic and ginger in a food processor or blender and chop finely. Add the yogurt and strain in the lemon juice from the chicken. Purée, then pour over the chicken. Cover and put in the refrigerator for 24 hours.

Remove the chicken pieces, reserving the marinade. Thread the chicken cubes on to kebab skewers and place them under a preheated grill. Grill as slowly as possible for 6–8 minutes until just cooked through. Remove the chicken from the skewers. Meanwhile, make the masala. Melt the ghee or butter in a wok, add the onion and garlic and fry for 4–5 minutes until soft. Sprinkle on the turmeric, chilli powder and cinnamon, stir well and fry for 1 minute. Add the cardamom, coriander and aniseed and stir-fry for 2 minutes, then add the reserved yogurt marinade. Mix well and bring to the boil. Add the chicken and cook for 5 minutes. Garnish with the chopped parsley and serve immediately.

187 Chicken biryani

188 Chicken tagine

Preparation time:
30 minutes, plus marinating

Cooking time:
about 1¼ hours

Oven temperature:
150°C (300°F) Gas Mark 2

Serves: 4–6

5 garlic cloves, crushed
8 cm (3 inches) fresh root ginger, grated
1 onion, chopped
1 teaspoon cloves
1 teaspoon black peppercorns
seeds from 3 cardamom pods
1 tablespoon coriander seeds
1 tablespoon cumin seeds
½ teaspoon turmeric
4 tablespoons vegetable oil or ghee
300 ml (½ pint) thick Greek yogurt
1.5 kg (3 lb) chicken, cut into 8 joints
10 saffron threads
300 ml (½ pint) hot milk
500 g (1 lb) basmati rice
1 cinnamon stick, broken up
2 bay leaves
6 cardamom pods, bruised
150 ml (¼ pint) Chicken Stock
75 g (3 oz) sultanas
50 g (2 oz) toasted almonds

Blend the garlic, ginger, onion, cloves, peppercorns, cardamom seeds, coriander and cumin seeds and turmeric into a paste, and fry it in half the oil for 2–3 minutes. Leave to cool, stir in the yogurt and spread over the chicken. Cover and leave to marinate for at least 3 hours. Heat the remaining oil in a large casserole. Remove the chicken from the marinade, brown on all sides, remove from the heat and add the leftover marinade.

Soak the saffron in the milk. Put the rice into a saucepan, cover with water and bring to the boil. Simmer for 5 minutes. Drain and place on top of the chicken. Add the cinnamon stick, bay leaves and cardamon pods. Pour the milk and the stock over the rice, cover the casserole with a lid and cook in a preheated oven, 150°C (300°F), Gas Mark 2, for 1 hour.

Put the sultanas and almonds on top of the rice for the last 10 minutes of cooking. Serve garnished with silver leaf, and fried onion, if liked.

Preparation time:
15 minutes

Cooking time:
about 1¼ hours

Serves: 4

2 tablespoons olive oil
1 Spanish onion, chopped
4 garlic cloves, crushed
1 red chilli, deseeded and finely chopped
1 tablespoon grated fresh root ginger
1½ teaspoons ground cumin
1½ teaspoons ground coriander
1 teaspoon ground allspice
4 chicken legs
750 ml (1¼ pints) Chicken Stock (see introduction)
1 red pepper, cored, deseeded and sliced
1 courgette, sliced
2 carrots, sliced
375 g (12 oz) canned chickpeas
chopped coriander and coriander sprigs, to garnish
couscous, to serve

Heat the oil in a saucepan. Add the onion, garlic, chilli and ginger and cook over a medium heat, stirring frequently, until the onion has softened and is lightly browned. Add the cumin, coriander and allspice and stir for 1 minute, then add the chicken. Pour in the stock and heat to simmering point. Cover and simmer over a low heat for 30 minutes.

Add the red pepper, courgette and carrots. Cover and continue to simmer for 30 minutes or until the vegetables are tender.

Add the chickpeas to the saucepan and simmer, uncovered, for 5 minutes more.

Make a bed of couscous on a large, warmed serving dish. Put the chicken in the centre. Scoop the vegetables from the casserole using a slotted spoon and add to the chicken. Pour the cooking juices over the chicken and couscous. Scatter over the chopped coriander, garnish with coriander sprigs and serve immediately.

Preparation time:	1 tablespoon vegetable oil
5 minutes	4 boneless duck breasts
	4 tablespoons balsamic vinegar
Cooking time:	75 g (3 oz) frozen cranberries, defrosted
25 minutes	50 g (2 oz) brown sugar
	salt and pepper
Serves: 4	freshly cooked vegetables (such as potatoes and asparagus), to serve

Heat the oil in a heavy-based frying pan. Add the duck breasts, skin side down, and cook over a moderate heat for 5 minutes. Reduce the heat and cook for a further 10 minutes. Drain off the excess oil.

Turn the duck breasts over and add the balsamic vinegar together with the cranberries and sugar. Season to taste and cook for a further 10 minutes.

Serve the duck breast with the sauce spooned over, accompanied by freshly cooked vegetables.

COOK'S NOTES Balsamic vinegar is a sweet, rich dark brown vinegar that comes from the Modena region of Northern Italy. It is aged in oak barrels for many years, which gives it its mellow flavour and colour.

Preparation time:	2–2.5 kg (4–5 lb) duckling with giblets
15 minutes, plus	coarse salt, for sprinkling
standing and chilling	500 ml (17 fl oz) thick coconut milk
	4 kaffir lime leaves, plus extra to garnish
Cooking time:	2–3 tablespoons Thai green curry paste
1½–1¾ hours	2–3 fresh green chillies, deseeded and sliced
Serves: 4–6	Thai fish sauce, to taste
	sliced red chillies, to garnish

Dry the duck thoroughly with kitchen paper. Sprinkle the skin generously with coarse salt and set it aside for 15 minutes.

Brush off the salt and chop the duck into 5 cm (2 inch) pieces. Heat a wok or frying pan over medium-high heat. Add a few pieces of duck and brown them thoroughly. Remove with a slotted spoon and drain on kitchen paper. Brown the remaining duck pieces in the same way. Discard the rendered fat from the wok and wipe it clean.

Reduce the heat to moderate. Skim the coconut cream from the top of the coconut milk and bring to the boil in the wok, then add the lime leaves and curry paste. Reduce the heat and cook, stirring constantly, until the oil begins to separate. Add the duck pieces, turn to cover evenly with the sauce then cook gently for 5 minutes.

Add the coconut milk, bring just to the boil, then reduce the heat to very low. Simmer, stirring occasionally, for about 1–1¼ hours until the duck is tender. Add water if necessary to maintain a smooth, creamy consistency. Remove from the heat, transfer to a bowl and allow to cool. Cover and chill overnight.

Skin the excess fat from the curry, then return to the wok, stir in the chillies and season with Thai fish sauce. Simmer for 5 minutes or until heated through. Transfer to a warmed serving dish, garnish with sliced red chillies and shredded lime leaves and serve immediately.

191 Turkey burgers with sun-dried tomatoes

192 Turkey ragoût

Preparation time:
20 minutes

Cooking time:
20–25 minutes

Serves: 4

8 sun-dried tomato halves in oil, drained
  and chopped
500 g (1 lb) minced turkey
1 tablespoon chopped tarragon
½ red onion, finely chopped
¼ teaspoon paprika
¼ teaspoon salt
4 slices of smoked pancetta or rindless
  streaky bacon, halved

TO SERVE:
4 ciabatta rolls
shredded radicchio
shredded Cos lettuce

Preparation time:
10 minutes

Cooking time:
1 hour 50 minutes

Oven temperature:
180°C (350°F)
Gas Mark 4

Serves: 4

1 turkey drumstick, 625 g (1¼ lb)
4 garlic cloves
15 baby onions or shallots
3 carrots, diagonally sliced
300 ml (½ pint) red wine
2 thyme sprigs
2 bay leaves
2 tablespoons chopped flat leaf parsley
1 teaspoon port wine jelly
1 teaspoon wholegrain mustard
salt and pepper

Place the sun-dried tomatoes, turkey and tarragon in a blender or food processor and blend until smooth. Spoon the mixture into a bowl and stir in the onion. Add the paprika and salt. Mix well, divide into 4 portions and shape into burgers. Stretch two strips of pancetta or bacon over each burger and secure with cocktail sticks soaked in water for 30 minutes.

Cook the burgers on an oiled barbecue grill or under a preheated hot grill for 20–25 minutes, turning frequently. Serve immediately in the ciabatta rolls with shredded lettuce.

Carefully remove the skin from the turkey drumstick. Once the skin is removed make a few slashes in the meat. Finely slice 1 garlic clove into slivers and push these into the slashes. Crush the remaining garlic. Put the drumstick in a large flameproof casserole or roasting tin with the onions, carrots, garlic, red wine, thyme and bay leaves. Season well and cover with a lid.

Cook in a preheated oven, 180°C (350°F), Gas Mark 4, for about 1¾ hours.

Remove the turkey and vegetables and keep hot. Bring the sauce to the boil on the hob, discarding the bay leaves. Add the parsley, port wine jelly and mustard. Boil for 5 minutes, until slightly thickened and check and adjust the seasoning. Carve the turkey and serve with the juices and the vegetables.

COOK'S NOTES Tarragon is a delicately flavoured herb that is best used fresh. It goes particularly well with poultry, such as turkey or chicken. French tarragon is much more highly regarded than Russian tarragon as it has a stronger scent and flavour.

9   Desserts

193 Fruit salad

194 Griddled pineapple with hazelnuts

Preparation time:
30 minutes

Cooking time:
5 minutes

Serves: 4

125 g (4 oz) watermelon, deseeded and sliced
1 galia melon, deseeded and sliced
1 large banana, sliced
125 g (4 oz) pineapple, peeled and sliced
1 orange, segmented
juice of ½ lime
25 g (1 oz) granulated sugar
50 ml (2 fl oz) water
25 g (1 oz) pecan nuts, chopped, halved or whole, to garnish

Reserve 5 watermelon slices and dice the rest. Mix all the fruit except for the watermelon slices in a heat-resistant bowl with the lime juice.

Purée and strain 1 slice of watermelon. Dissolve the sugar in the water over a low heat and bring to the boil. Add the puréed watermelon to the syrup and pour it over the fruit.

Refrigerate until cold. Serve with watermelon slices and garnish with pecan nuts.

Preparation time:
5 minutes

Cooking time:
5 minutes

Serves: 4

1 pineapple, peeled, halved lengthways and sliced
125 g (4 oz) roasted hazelnuts, chopped
125 g (4 oz) crème fraîche

Heat a griddle pan until hot. Place the pineapple slices on the griddle pan and cook for 1–2 minutes on each side.

Mix the hazelnuts into the crème fraîche. Serve the griddled pineapple with the nutty crème fraîche spooned over it.

COOK'S NOTES Do not move the pineapple slices around while griddling, or you will not achieve the attractive dark stripes. Griddling caramelizes the sugar in the fruit, bringing out the natural sweetness.

Preparation time:	2 ripe pears, peeled, cored and quartered
5 minutes, plus	250 ml (8 fl oz) freshly squeezed orange
chilling	juice
	50 ml (2 fl oz) dark rum
Cooking time:	½ cinnamon stick
10 minutes	175 g (6 oz) seedless black grapes,
	halved
Serves: 4	½ firm honeydew melon, peeled,
	deseeded and cut into large chunks
	ground cinnamon, to dust (optional)
	dessert biscuits, to serve

Put the pears, orange juice, rum and cinnamon stick into a large saucepan. Cover and simmer for 5 minutes. Add the remaining fruit and simmer for a further 5 minutes.

Remove from the heat and transfer to a bowl. Chill overnight and remove the cinnamon before serving. Decorate with a dusting of ground cinnamon, if liked, and serve with dessert biscuits.

Preparation time:	4 medium cooking apples, cored
20 minutes	1 tablespoon chopped nuts, toasted
	1 tablespoon chopped dates
Cooking time:	juice of ½ lemon
45 minutes	2 tablespoons clear honey, plus extra
	for pouring
Oven temperature:	½ teaspoon ground cinnamon
190°C (375°F)	
Gas Mark 5	
Serves: 4	

Wash the apples, peel the top half and arrange them in an ovenproof dish. Put the remaining ingredients in a bowl, mix them together and use the mixture to fill the centres of the apples.

Pour a little more honey over the apples and cook them, covered, in a preheated oven, 190°C (375°F), Gas Mark 5, for about 45 minutes.

COOK'S NOTES Serve these hot juicy apples with double cream, crème fraîche or thin homemade custard.

197 Plum and almond tart

Preparation time:
20 minutes, plus chilling

Cooking time:
50 minutes

Oven temperature:
220°C (425°F) Gas Mark 7

Serves: **6–8**

SWEET PASTRY:
250 g (8 oz) plain flour
pinch of salt
75 g (3 oz) caster sugar
1 large egg
125 g (4 oz) butter, softened
1½ teaspoons orange-flower water

FILLING:
1 tablespoon ground almonds
500 g (1 lb) dessert plums, halved and stoned
50 g (2 oz) soft brown sugar
½ teaspoon ground cinnamon
2 tablespoons blanched flaked almonds
cream, to serve

Sift the flour, salt and caster sugar into a bowl and make a well in the centre. Add the egg, butter and orange-flower water and work the ingredients together. Knead the dough lightly and quickly until it is smooth. Cover with clingfilm and chill for 30 minutes.

Roll out the pastry and use to line a 20 cm (8 inch) flan tin. Prick the base with a fork and bake blind in a preheated oven, 220°C (425°F), Gas Mark 7, for 10 minutes.

Sprinkle the ground almonds in the cooked pastry case and arrange the plum halves on top, skin side up, overlapping them if necessary.

Mix together the sugar, cinnamon and flaked almonds and sprinkle over the plums.

Return the tart to the oven and bake for 40 minutes. Serve hot or cold with cream.

COOK'S NOTES Handle this pastry as little as possible to keep it cool, using only your fingertips to combine the ingredients. Try not to stretch the pastry as you are lining the tin or it will shrink back during cooking.

198 Lemon tart with plums

Preparation time:
30 minutes, plus chilling

Cooking time:
40–45 minutes

Oven temperature:
190°C (350°F) Gas Mark 5

Serves: **6–8**

SHORTCRUST PASTRY:
175 g (6 oz) plain flour
75 g (3 oz) chilled butter, diced
50 g (2 oz) caster sugar
1 egg, beaten

FILLING:
50 g (2 oz) butter, at room temperature
50 g (2 oz) caster sugar
50 g (2 oz) semolina
grated rind of 1 lemon
1 egg, beaten
750 g (1½ lb) ripe plums, halved and stoned
4 tablespoons apricot jam
whipped cream, to serve

Sift the flour into a bowl, add the diced butter and rub in with the fingertips until the mixture resembles fine breadcrumbs. Stir in the caster sugar and beaten egg and mix to a firm dough, adding a little iced water if necessary. Knead the dough briefly on a lightly floured surface, then wrap in clingfilm and chill for 30 minutes.

Roll out the pastry and use it to line a 23 cm (9 inch) flan tin. Prick the pastry base with a fork.

To make the filling, mix together the butter and sugar in a bowl until light and fluffy. Beat in the semolina, lemon rind and beaten egg and spread the mixture over the pastry base. Arrange the plum halves over the top, cut sides down.

Bake the tart in a preheated oven, 190°C (375°F), Gas Mark 5, for 40–45 minutes or until the pastry is browned and the filling golden and set. Warm the jam in a small saucepan, then press it through a sieve into a bowl. Brush the apricot glaze over the top of the tart. Serve warm or cold, with lightly whipped cream.

199 Lemon and bay custards

Preparation time: **5 minutes, plus infusing**	**12 bay leaves, bruised**
	2 tablespoons grated lemon rind
	150 ml (¼ pint) double cream
	4 eggs
Cooking time: **about 1 hour**	**1 egg yolk**
	150 g (5 oz) caster sugar
	100 ml (3½ fl oz) lemon juice
Oven temperature: **120°C (250°F) Gas Mark ½**	
Serves: **4**	

Put the bay leaves, lemon rind and cream in a small saucepan and heat gently. When the mixture reaches boiling point, remove it from the heat and set aside for 2 hours to infuse.

Whisk together the eggs, egg yolk and sugar until the mixture is pale and creamy and then whisk in the lemon juice. Strain the cream mixture through a fine sieve into the egg mixture and stir until combined.

Pour the custard into 4 individual ramekins and place on a baking sheet. Bake in a preheated oven, 120°C (250°F), Gas Mark ½, for 50 minutes or until the custards are almost set in the middle. Leave until cold and chill until required. Return to room temperature before serving.

COOK'S NOTES Bay leaves are rarely used in sweet dishes, yet they add a lovely musky fragrance to these creamy custards.

200 Lemon cheesecake with blueberries

Preparation time: **30 minutes, plus chilling**	**500 g (1 lb) skimmed ricotta**
	2 large eggs
	75 g (3 oz) sugar
	150 g (5 oz) natural yogurt
Cooking time: **about 1 hour**	**4 tablespoons lemon juice**
	grated rind of 2 lemons
	2 tablespoons plain flour
Oven temperature: **190°C (375°F) Gas Mark 5**	**2 teaspoons vanilla essence**
	2 egg whites
	150 g (5 oz) natural fromage frais
Serves: **10**	**300 g (10 oz) fresh, frozen and defrosted or canned blueberries or other soft fruit**

CRUST:
125 g (4 oz) digestive biscuits, crushed
2 tablespoons sugar
1 teaspoon ground cinnamon
15 g (½ oz) butter or margarine, melted
1 egg white

To make the crust, mix together the biscuits, sugar, cinnamon and butter or margarine in a bowl. In a separate bowl whisk the egg white until it is frothy. Stir the egg white into the crumb mixture. Press the mixture into the bottom of a 23 cm (9 inch) spring-form tin. Bake in a preheated oven, 190°C (375°F) Gas Mark 5, for 7–10 minutes until lightly browned. Allow to cool.

Put the ricotta and whole eggs in a blender or food processor and blend until smooth. Beat together the cheese and egg mixture, sugar, yogurt, lemon juice and rind, flour and vanilla essence until well mixed. In a separate bowl beat the egg whites to form soft peaks then fold into the cheese mixture. Spread over the crust and bake in the oven for 50–55 minutes until the centre is firm to the touch.

Run a knife around the edge of the cake to loosen it and leave to cool. Remove the sides of the tin, cover the cheesecake and refrigerate for at least 2 hours or overnight. Just before serving, spread the top with fromage frais and cover with blueberries or other fruit.

201 Lemon meringue pie

Preparation time:
15 minutes, plus chilling

Cooking time:
about 1 hour

Oven temperature:
220°C (425°F) Gas Mark 7, then 190°C (375°F) Gas Mark 5

Serves: **6–8**

SHORTCRUST PASTRY:
175 g (6 oz) plain flour
100 g (3½ oz) chilled butter, diced
25 g caster sugar
1 egg yolk
2–3 tablespoons cold water

FILLING:
grated rind and juice of 3 lemons
175 g (6 oz) caster sugar
3 eggs, beaten
250 g (8 oz) butter, diced

MERINGUE:
3 egg whites
75 g (3 oz) caster sugar

Sift the flour into a bowl, add the butter and rub in with the fingertips until the mixture resembles fine breadcrumbs. Stir in the sugar and gradually work in the egg yolk and water to make a firm dough. Knead the dough briefly on a lightly floured surface. Wrap it in clingfilm and chill for 30 minutes. Roll out the pastry and use it to line a 23 cm (9 inch) flan tin. Prick the pastry base with a fork and chill for 20 minutes. Bake the pastry case blind in a preheated oven, 220°C (425°F), Gas Mark 7, for 10 minutes. Remove the paper and beans and bake for a further 10–12 minutes until the pastry is crisp and golden. Remove from the oven and reduce the temperature to 190°C (375°F), Gas Mark 5.

To make the filling, put the lemon rind and juice in a saucepan with the sugar and eggs, place over a very low heat and stir well. Add the butter to the pan, one cube at a time. Continue stirring over a low heat, until all the butter has been incorporated. Pour the lemon mixture into the prepared pastry case and return to the oven for about 10 minutes or until the filling is just set. Remove from the oven and allow to cool.

Beat the egg whites until they form stiff peaks. Gradually beat in the caster sugar. Pile the meringue on top of the filling and bake in the oven for 12–15 minutes or until the meringue is browned. Serve hot or cold.

202 Key lime pie

Preparation time:
30 minutes, plus chilling

Cooking time:
15–20 minutes

Oven temperature:
160°C (325°F) Gas Mark 3

Serves: **8**

PIE CRUST:
175 g (6 oz) digestive biscuits, crushed
125 g (4 oz) caster sugar
75 g (3 oz) butter, melted

FILLING:
3 eggs, separated
125 g (4 oz) condensed milk
125 ml (4 fl oz) lime juice
1 tablespoon lemon juice
2 teaspoons grated lime zest
2 tablespoons caster sugar

TOPPING:
250 ml (8 fl oz) double cream
1 tablespoon icing sugar, sifted
3 drops of vanilla extract
lime slices, to decorate (optional)

Mix together the digestive biscuit crumbs, the sugar and the melted butter and press over the bottom and up the sides of a 23 cm (9 inch) spring-form tin. Put in the refrigerator to chill.

Lightly beat the egg yolks together until creamy. Add the condensed milk, lime and lemon juices and lime zest and beat until well mixed and slightly thickened. In another bowl beat the egg whites until frothy. Add the sugar and continue beating until the meringue holds soft peaks. Fold gently but thoroughly into the lime mixture using a large metal spoon.

Spoon the filling into the crumb crust and smooth the top. Bake in a preheated oven, 160°C (325°F), Gas Mark 3, for 15–20 minutes or until the filling is just firm and lightly browned on top. When cool, refrigerate the pie for at least 3 hours until it is well chilled.

Whip the cream until it begins to thicken. Add the sugar and vanilla extract and continue whipping until quite thick but not stiff. Spread the cream over the top of the chilled pie. Remove the sides of the tin just before serving and serve chilled, decorated with lime slices, if liked.

203 Lime and raspberry cheesecakes

Preparation time:
10 minutes

Serves: **4**

6 ginger biscuits, lightly crushed
200 g (7 oz) cream cheese
200 g (7 oz) fromage frais
3 drops of vanilla extract
1 tablespoon caster sugar
grated rind and juice of 1 lime
125 g (4 oz) raspberries
lime wedges, to garnish

Divide the biscuits among 4 small glass dishes.

In a bowl mix together the cream cheese, fromage frais, vanilla extract, sugar and the lime rind and juice.

Spoon the mixture over the biscuits. Top with the raspberries and serve immediately, garnished with a lime wedge.

COOK'S NOTES To crush the biscuits, put them in a plastic food storage bag and crush them with a rolling pin. Alternatively, whizz them quickly in a blender or food processor.

204 No-bake lime and blueberry cheesecake

Preparation time:
20 minutes, plus chilling

Serves: **4**

50 g (2 oz) butter
2 tablespoons golden syrup
150 g (5 oz) malted milk biscuits, finely crushed

FILLING:
250 g (8 oz) mascarpone
200 g (7 oz) fromage frais
50 g (2 oz) caster sugar, sifted
grated rind and juice of 2 limes
150 ml (¼ pint) double cream

TO DECORATE:
250 g (8 oz) strawberries, halved or sliced, if large
125 g (4 oz) fresh blueberries
sifted icing sugar (optional)

To make the base, melt the butter and syrup in a saucepan. Stir the biscuit crumbs into the butter mixture, mix well and press into the base of an 18 cm (7 inch) loose-bottomed, fluted flan tin. Put in the refrigerator to chill.

Beat the mascarpone in a bowl to soften, then stir in the fromage frais, sugar and lime rind. Gradually beat in the lime juice.

In a second bowl whisk the cream until it forms soft peaks, then fold into the mascarpone mixture. Spoon the creamy filling on to the biscuit base and swirl the top with the back of a spoon. Refrigerate for 3 hours or longer, if preferred.

Carefully remove the cheesecake from the tin, decorate with berries and a dusting of icing sugar, if liked.

COOK'S NOTES You could add lemon, or a combination of lemon and lime, or even orange juice to this cheesecake.

Preparation time:	250 g (8 oz) strawberries
20 minutes, plus	**8 digestive biscuits**
chilling	**4 teaspoons strawberry jam**
	250 g (8 oz) cream cheese
Serves: **4**	**2 teaspoons icing sugar**
	icing sugar, to decorate

Hull and slice the strawberries, reserving 4 for decoration. Fan the 4 reserved strawberries.

Spread a digestive biscuit with 1 teaspoon of the strawberry jam. Beat the cream cheese to soften and stir in the icing sugar, then spread one-quarter of it over the biscuit. Lay a few strawberry slices on top of the cream cheese, then top with a second biscuit. Lay a fanned strawberry on top and dust with icing sugar. Repeat to make 3 more shortcakes. Chill for at least 1 hour before serving.

Preparation time:	CRUMB CASE:
30 minutes, plus	**125 g (4 oz) butter**
chilling	**250 g (8 oz) digestive biscuits, crushed**
Serves: **6–8**	FILLING:
	175 g (6 oz) butter
	175 g (6 oz) caster sugar
	425 g (14 oz) can condensed milk
	2 bananas
	1 tablespoon lemon juice
	150 ml (¼ pint) whipping cream
	25 g (1 oz) dark chocolate, grated

To make the crumb case, melt the butter in a saucepan and stir in the biscuit crumbs. Press the mixture evenly over the base and sides of a deep 20 cm (8 inch) round flan tin. Chill until firm.

To make the filling, put the butter and sugar in a saucepan and heat gently, stirring, until the butter has melted. Stir in the condensed milk and bring to the boil. Lower the heat and simmer for 5 minutes, stirring occasionally, until the mixture becomes a caramel colour. Pour into the base, leave to cool, then chill until set.

Slice the bananas and toss them in the lemon juice. Reserve one-quarter of the bananas for decoration and spread the rest over the filling. Whip the cream and spread it over the top. Decorate with the reserved bananas and sprinkle with chocolate.

COOK'S NOTES Even if you are on a diet you can enjoy strawberry shortcake by using low-fat cream cheese and low-sugar biscuits and jam in this recipe.

Preparation time:	**1 egg yolk**
15 minutes, plus	**2 tablespoons caster sugar**
chilling	**1 teaspoon vanilla extract**
	250 g (8 oz) mascarpone
Serves: **4**	**125 ml (4 fl oz) strong black coffee**
	2 tablespoons brandy
	1 tablespoon cocoa powder
	16 amaretti biscuits
	flake chocolate or cocoa powder, to decorate

In a large bowl beat the egg yolk and sugar until smooth. Stir in the vanilla extract and mascarpone until thoroughly combined, then set the mixture aside.

Mix the coffee, brandy and cocoa. Break up the amaretti biscuits and stir them into the coffee mixture, then divide half the mixture among 4 bowls or glasses.

Spoon half the mascarpone mixture over the biscuit mixture, add the remaining biscuit mixture and top with the rest of the mascarpone. Dust lightly with cocoa or crumble flake chocolate over the top. Chill before serving.

Preparation time:	**2 oranges**
25 minutes	**40 g (1½ oz) butter**
	50 g (2 oz) rice flour
Cooking time:	**25 g (1 oz) plus 1 tablespoon caster sugar**
about 20 minutes	**100 ml (3½ fl oz) milk**
	2 eggs, separated
Serves: **4–6**	**oil, for frying**
	2 tablespoons lemon juice
	2 tablespoons orange liqueur (optional)
	6 scoops vanilla ice cream, to serve

Finely grate the rind from 1 orange. Melt 15 g (½ oz) of the butter. Put the flour, orange rind, melted butter, 1 tablespoon of the sugar, the milk and the egg yolks in a mixing bowl and whisk until smooth.

In a separate bowl whisk the egg whites until they are frothy and just beginning to hold their shape. Add to the other bowl and stir in until combined (the mixture should be foamy but still quite loose).

Heat a little oil in a medium-sized crêpe pan, drain off the excess oil and pour a little of the batter into the pan so that it spreads into a round about 15 cm (6 inches) in diameter. (If the batter is so thick that it doesn't run, spread it with the back of a dessertspoon.) As soon as it is golden on the underside, turn the pancake with a fish slice and cook until set enough to slide out of the pan. Keep the pancakes warm while you make the rest, brushing the pan with a little more oil each time.

Squeeze the juice from the 2 oranges. Melt the remaining butter and sugar in a frying pan until the sugar has dissolved. Add the orange and lemon juice and let the mixture bubble for about 2 minutes or until it is syrupy. Stir in the liqueur if using.

Fold the pancakes into quarters and arrange on serving plates. Pour the sauce over and serve immediately with ice cream.

COOK'S NOTES **If you don't have any brandy, you could use dark rum instead.**

209 Crème caramel

210 Panna cotta with blueberry compôte

Preparation time:
15 minutes, plus chilling

Cooking time:
45 minutes

Oven temperature:
150°C (300°F)
Gas Mark 2

Serves: **4**

500 ml (17 fl oz) milk
1 vanilla pod, split lengthways
4 eggs
50 g (2 oz) sugar

CARAMEL:
50 g (2 oz) sugar
1 tablespoon water
1 teaspoon lemon juice

Preparation time:
30 minutes, plus chilling

Serves: **8**

600 ml (1 pint) double cream
1 vanilla pod, split lengthways
4 strips of lemon rind
50 g (2 oz) caster sugar
1½ teaspoons gelatine
2 tablespoons Amaretto di Saronno liqueur

BLUEBERRY COMPÔTE:
250 g (8 oz) blueberries
50 g (2 oz) caster sugar
1 tablespoon lemon juice
2 tablespoons water

Put the milk and vanilla pod into a heavy saucepan and bring to the boil. Remove from the heat and leave for 5 minutes to infuse. Put the eggs and sugar in a bowl and whisk until thoroughly combined. Discard the vanilla pod and whisk the milk into the egg and sugar mixture.

Next make the caramel. Put the sugar, water and lemon juice into a small saucepan and cook over a moderate heat, stirring well until the sugar dissolves. As soon as it turns a rich golden-caramel colour remove the pan from the heat.

Pour the caramel into four small moulds or a 1 litre (1¾ pint) charlotte mould. Rotate the moulds quickly so that the caramel coats the base and sides evenly.

Strain the custard through a fine sieve, then pour into the moulds and stand them in a bain marie or roasting tin half-filled with boiling water. Cook in a preheated oven, 150°C (300°F), Gas Mark 2, for about 45 minutes or until set. Leave to cool and then chill in the refrigerator before unmoulding.

Heat 450 ml (¾ pint) of the cream in a saucepan with the vanilla pod, lemon rind and sugar until it almost reaches boiling point, then strain through a fine sieve.

Soak the gelatine in the liqueur for 1 minute, then heat very gently until the gelatine dissolves. Make sure that you do not let the gelatine boil because this destabilizes it. Stir a little of the vanilla cream into the gelatine and then pour this back into the rest of the vanilla cream.

Whisk the remaining cream until it forms soft peaks and fold it into the cooled vanilla cream. Pour into eight 150 ml (¼ pint) moulds and chill for 2–3 hours or until set.

Meanwhile, put the blueberries, sugar, lemon juice and water in a saucepan and heat gently until the blueberries soften and the liquid becomes a little syrupy. Leave to cool.

Unmould the set panna cotta by briefly immersing the base and sides of the moulds in hot water. Invert on to plates and spoon the blueberry compote around them.

COOK'S NOTES To unmould crème caramel, dip the base of the moulds into a bowl of hot water for 30 seconds and then turn them out on to a serving plate.

211 Vanilla crème brûlée

212 Nectarine brûlée

Preparation time:
20 minutes, plus
infusing and chilling

1 vanilla pod, split lengthways
600 ml (1 pint) double cream
8 egg yolks
50 g (2 oz) caster sugar
3 tablespoons icing sugar, sifted

Cooking time:
20–30 minutes

Oven temperature:
180°C (350°F)
Gas Mark 4

Serves: **6**

Put the vanilla pod into a saucepan. Pour the cream into the pan and bring it slowly almost to the boil. Take off the heat and leave to stand for 15 minutes for the vanilla flavour to infuse.

Lift the vanilla pod out of the cream and holding it against the side of the saucepan, scrape the black seeds into the cream. Discard the pod.

Fork together the eggs and sugar in a bowl. Reheat the cream then gradually mix it into the eggs and sugar. Tip the cream mixture back into the saucepan and heat gently, stirring continuously for 2–3 minutes until the custard is just beginning to thicken and thinly coats the back of the spoon.

Stand six ovenproof ramekins or custard pots in a roasting tin then divide the custard among them. Pour warm water around the dishes to come halfway up the sides. Cook in a preheated oven, 180°C (350°F), Gas Mark 4, for 20–25 minutes until the custards are just set and still have a slight softness or wobble at the centre.

Leave the ramekins or pots to cool in the water then lift them out and chill in the refrigerator for 3–4 hours. About 20–30 minutes before serving, sprinkle the tops with sifted icing sugar. Caramelize using a blowtorch then leave at room temperature.

Preparation time:
10 minutes

500 g (1 lb) nectarines, pitted and sliced
4 tablespoons orange liqueur, plus extra
   to flavour fruit

Cooking time:
10–15 minutes

350 ml (12 fl oz) soured cream
pinch of grated nutmeg
1 teaspoon vanilla essence

Serves: **6**

125 g (4 oz) light brown sugar

Put the nectarines in a saucepan and add just enough water to cover. Poach over a low heat for 5–10 minutes or until tender. Drain and divide among 6 individual ramekins. Stir in a little orange liqueur.

Beat together the soured cream, nutmeg, vanilla and remaining orange liqueur until blended. Spoon over the nectarine slices, then scatter the brown sugar over the top in a thick layer. Grill under a preheated hot grill until the sugar caramelizes.

COOK'S NOTES If you prefer, use fresh apricots, peaches or pineapple instead of nectarines. Double cream may be used instead of soured cream.

213 Apple and fig crumble   214 Baked plum crumble

Preparation time: **20 minutes**	**125 g (4 oz) wholemeal plain flour** **50 g (2 oz) butter or margarine** **50 g (2 oz) brown sugar**
Cooking time: **25–30 minutes**	**500 g (1 lb) cooking apples (such as** **Bramleys), peeled, cored and sliced** **6 dried or fresh figs, diced**
Oven temperature: **180°C (350°F)** **Gas Mark 4**	**grated rind and juice of 1 lemon** **1 teaspoon ground cinnamon**
Serves: **6**	

Sift the flour into a large bowl and add the bran left in the sieve. Lightly rub in the butter or margarine until the mixture forms coarse crumbs. Stir in the sugar.

Arrange the fruit in a 1.2 litre (2 pint) ovenproof dish, add the lemon rind and juice and the cinnamon. Spoon the crumble mixture over the fruit and bake in a preheated oven, 180°C (350°F), Gas Mark 4, for 25–30 minutes or until golden-brown. Serve warm.

Preparation time: **10 minutes**	**500 g (1 lb) plums, halved and stoned** **2 tablespoons runny honey** **2.5 cm (1 inch) fresh root ginger, grated**
Cooking time: **35 minutes**	**pinch of cinnamon** **grated rind and juice of 1 orange** **custard or fromage frais, to serve**
Oven temperature: **200°C (400°F)** **Gas Mark 6**	TOPPING: **125 g (4 oz) sugar-free muesli** **50 g (2 oz) digestive biscuits, crushed**
Serves: **6**	**50 g (2 oz) plain flour** **25 g (1 oz) butter or margarine**

Arrange the plums in an ovenproof dish. Top with the honey, ginger, cinnamon and orange juice and rind. Cook in a preheated oven, 200°C (400°F), Gas Mark 6, for 15 minutes.

Meanwhile, put all the remaining ingredients into a bowl and mix to form the crumb topping.

Remove the plums from the oven and scatter the crumble mixture over. Continue cooking for 20 minutes. Serve with custard or fromage frais.

COOK'S NOTES Always remember to use plenty of fruit – 500–750 g (1–1½ lb) – and sweeten sour fruit by mixing with sweeter fruit, or some dried fruit. Try the following combinations: plum and blackberry, rhubarb and strawberry, cranberry and apple or pear and blackcurrant.

215 Mango mousse

Preparation time:
15 minutes, plus setting

Cooking time:
2 minutes

Serves: **6**

2 mangoes
75 g (3 oz) icing sugar, sifted
juice of 1 lime or ½ lemon
2 teaspoons gelatine, soaked in
  2 tablespoons cold water
300 ml (½ pint) double cream, whipped
lime or lemon rind strips, to decorate

Cut the mangoes in half lengthways, scoop out the flesh and put it in a blender or food processor. Add the icing sugar and lime or lemon juice and blend until smooth.

Heat the gelatine gently until it has dissolved. Cool slightly, then blend it into the mango purée with the whipped cream. Pour into individual glass bowls and leave to set.

Serve decorated with strips of lime or lemon rind.

216 Chocolate mousse with whipped cream

Preparation time:
15 minutes, plus chilling

Serves: **8**

4 eggs, separated
125 g (4 oz) caster sugar
125 g (4 oz) plain chocolate, broken into
  small pieces
3 tablespoons water
300 ml (½ pint) double cream, plus extra
  to decorate
chocolate curls, to decorate

Put the egg yolks and sugar in a bowl and whisk with an electric beater until the mixture is thick and fluffy

Melt the chocolate with the water in a heatproof bowl over a pan of hot water. Remove from the heat and cool slightly.

Whisk this into the egg mixture. Whip the cream until it will stand in soft peaks, then carefully fold it into the chocolate mixture.

Whisk the egg whites until they form stiff peaks. Carefully fold 1 tablespoon into the mousse, then fold in the remainder.

Pour the mousse mixture into 8 individual dishes and chill. Serve decorated with whipped cream and chocolate curls.

COOK'S NOTES These mousses can be frozen until required. Pour the mousse mixture into freezer-proof dishes, cover with clingfilm, wrap in polythene bags, then seal, label and freeze for up to 3 months. To serve, put in the refrigerator for 10 minutes to allow them to soften slightly.

217 Chocolate semi-freddo

218 Double chocolate chip ice cream

Preparation time:	250 g (8 oz) mascarpone
10 minutes, plus	2 tablespoons brandy
freezing	2 tablespoons fine ground espresso coffee
Serves: 5–6	25 g (1 oz) icing sugar
	75 g (3 oz) bitter or plain chocolate, grated
	5 tablespoons single cream
	300 ml (½ pint) double cream

TO DECORATE:
coffee liqueur (optional)
lightly whipped cream

Beat the mascarpone in a bowl with the brandy, espresso coffee and icing sugar. Reserve 1 tablespoon of the grated chocolate and stir the remainder, together with the single cream, into the mixture.

Whip the double cream until it is just peaking and fold into the mascarpone mixture with a large metal spoon. Turn the mixture into a freezer-proof container and freeze for 2–3 hours.

To serve, use a metal spoon to scoop the semi-freddo into serving glasses or coffee cups. Drizzle with a little coffee-flavoured liqueur, if liked, and decorate with lightly whipped cream and sprinkles of the reserved grated chocolate.

Preparation time:	300 ml (½ pint) milk
15 minutes, plus	75 g (3 oz) soft dark brown sugar
cooling and freezing	75 g (3 oz) dark chocolate, broken into pieces
Cooking time:	2 eggs, beaten
15 minutes	½ teaspoon vanilla extract
	300 ml (½ pint) double cream
Serves: 4–6	75 g (3 oz) chocolate chips
	chocolate cookies, to serve (optional)

Put the milk, sugar and chocolate into a saucepan and heat gently until the chocolate has melted and the sugar dissolved. Pour the warm mixture over the beaten eggs, stirring constantly.

Return the mixture to the pan and cook over low heat, stirring constantly, until the custard begins to thicken slightly. Strain the mixture into a bowl and add the vanilla extract. Let it cool.

Whip the cream until it forms soft peaks, then whisk it into the cooled custard. Stir in the chocolate chips.

Turn the mixture into a freezer container, cover and freeze until firm. About 30 minutes before serving transfer the ice cream to the refrigerator to soften. Spoon or scoop the ice cream into individual dishes and serve with chocolate cookies, if liked.

COOK'S NOTES You could use any combination of white, milk and dark chocolate to make this ice cream. White chocolate ice cream with dark chocolate chips looks especially attractive.

219 Chocolate bread and butter pudding

Preparation time:	**200 g (7 oz) plain chocolate, broken**
10 minutes, plus	**into pieces**
standing	**50 g (2 oz) unsalted butter**
	½ teaspoon ground mixed spice
Cooking time:	**250 g (8 oz) brioche, cut into thin slices**
about 1 hour	**3 eggs**
	25 g (1 oz) caster sugar
Oven temperature:	**600 ml (1 pint) milk**
180°C (350°F)	**cocoa powder or icing sugar, for dusting**
Gas Mark 4	**single cream, to serve**

Serves: **6**

Put the chocolate in a heatproof bowl with half the butter and the mixed spice. Place over a saucepan of simmering water and leave until melted. Stir lightly.

Arrange about one-third of the brioche slices in greased individual ramekins or in a greased shallow 1.8 litre (3 pint) ovenproof dish.

Place spoonfuls of the chocolate sauce over the brioche. Cover with another third of the brioche slices and then the remaining sauce. Arrange the rest of the brioche on top.

Melt the remaining butter and mix thoroughly with the eggs, sugar and milk. Pour over the brioche and leave to stand for 30 minutes.

Bake in a preheated oven, 180°C (350°F), Gas Mark 4, for about 50 minutes until the crust is golden. Serve the pudding liberally dusted with cocoa powder or icing sugar and with the single cream.

COOK'S NOTES If you can't get brioche, use plain or chocolate croissants to make this delicious pudding.

220 Chocolate meringue stacks

Preparation time:	**2 egg whites**
40 minutes, plus	**125 g (4 oz) caster sugar**
cooling	**1 tablespoon cocoa powder, sifted**
Cooking time:	BITTER CHOCOLATE SAUCE:
about 2¼ hours	**175 g (6 oz) plain chocolate, broken into**
	pieces
Oven temperature:	**150 ml (¼ pint) water**
120°C (250°F)	**1 teaspoon instant coffee powder**
Gas Mark ½	**50 g (2 oz) sugar**
Makes: **8**	FILLING:
	150 ml (¼ pint) double cream
	2 tablespoons brandy
	1 teaspoon clear honey
	TO DECORATE:
	8 piped chocolate shapes
	grated chocolate

Whisk the egg whites until stiff, then whisk in the sugar, 1 tablespoon at a time, until the mixture holds its shape. Carefully fold in the cocoa. Line 2 baking sheets with baking parchment and carefully draw eight 8 cm (3 inch) and eight 5 cm (2 inch) circles on the paper. Put the meringue into a piping bag fitted with a 1 cm (½ inch) plain nozzle and pipe on to the circles to cover completely. Bake in a preheated oven, 120°C (250°F), Gas Mark ½, for 2 hours. Transfer to a wire rack to cool.

Put all the sauce ingredients in a saucepan, gently bring to the boil and simmer for 10 minutes.

To make the filling, whip together the cream, brandy and honey until the mixture thickens and holds its shape, then divide three-quarters of it between the large meringue circles. Cover with the small circles.

Serve the meringue stacks on individual plates and decorate with the remaining cream and the piped shapes. Spoon some bitter chocolate sauce around each one and sprinkle with a little grated chocolate.

Preparation time:
20 minutes

Cooking time:
50–55 minutes

Oven temperature:
**140°C (275°F)
Gas Mark 1**

Serves: **8**

3 chocolate flakes
4 egg whites
200 g (7 oz) caster sugar
1 teaspoon cornflour
1 teaspoon white wine vinegar
150 ml (¼ pint) double cream
325 g (11 oz) raspberries

SAUCE:
200 g (7 oz) plain chocolate, broken into pieces
4 tablespoons milk
3 tablespoons golden syrup
½ teaspoon vanilla essence
25 g (1 oz) unsalted butter

Line a large baking sheet with nonstick baking paper. Coarsely crumble the chocolate flakes into a bowl.

Whisk the egg whites in a large bowl until stiff. Gradually whisk in the sugar, 1 tablespoon at a time, until the meringue is stiff and glossy. Stir in the cornflour, vinegar and two-thirds of the crumbled chocolate flakes. Divide the mixture into eight mounds on the prepared baking sheet, spreading each one to about 8 cm (3 inches) in diameter and making a small dip in the centre. Bake in a preheated oven, 140°C (275°F), Gas Mark 1, for 45–50 minutes or until crisp. Set aside to cool.

To make the sauce, put the chocolate, milk, golden syrup and vanilla essence into a small saucepan and heat gently, stirring frequently until the chocolate has melted. Stir in the butter. Continue stirring until the sauce is smooth, then pour it into a jug.

Whip the cream, fold in the raspberries and spoon the mixture on to the meringues. Decorate with the remaining crumbled chocolate flakes and serve with the sauce.

Preparation time:
10 minutes, plus freezing

Serves: **4–6**

500 g (1 lb) raspberries, fresh or frozen
125 g (4 oz) sugar
300 ml (½ pint) water
2 egg whites

Defrost the raspberries at room temperature for 3–4 hours if you are using them from the freezer.

Pass the raspberries through a sieve. Put the sugar and water in a saucepan and stir over a gentle heat until the sugar has dissolved. Increase the heat and boil briskly, without stirring, for 8 minutes or until a syrup has formed. Allow to cool.

Stir the syrup into the raspberry purée and pour into an ice tray or shallow, rigid container.

Place in the freezer for 1 hour or until just smooth. Whisk the egg whites until stiff and fold into the raspberry mixture. Return to the container. Cover and seal, then return to the freezer.

To serve defrost, covered, in the refrigerator for 10–15 minutes, or microwave uncovered on Defrost for 2–3 minutes and allow to stand for 3 minutes before serving.

COOK'S NOTES If you have a glut of fresh raspberries from your garden, make this recipe and you will have a delicious sorbet available throughout the year at very little cost. For a special occasion, pour a little liqueur, such as Cointreau, over each serving.

223 Fresh lime sorbet

224 Plum sorbet

Preparation time:
20 minutes, plus freezing

Cooking time:
6 minutes

Serves: **4**

3 limes
175 g (6 oz) caster sugar
600 ml (1 pint) water
1 egg white, stiffly whisked

Pare the rinds from the limes with a potato peeler, reserve and squeeze the juice. Dissolve the sugar in the water and bring to the boil in a saucepan. Boil for 3 minutes. Add the lime rinds and boil briskly, uncovered, for a further 3 minutes. Remove the lime rinds, reserve, and set the mixture aside to cool.

Add the lime juice and strain into a freezer-proof container. Freeze until mushy. Stir thoroughly, mixing the sides into the centre, then carefully fold in the stiffly whisked egg white. Refreeze, covered, until firm.

Serve in individual bowls decorated with the reserved lime rinds.

Preparation time:
5 minutes

Cooking time:
55 minutes, plus freezing

Oven temperature:
200°C (400°F)
Gas Mark 6

Serves: **4**

750 g (1½ lb) Victoria plums, halved and stoned
250 g (8 oz) caster sugar
600 ml (1 pint) water
1 cinnamon stick
strip of lemon peel

TO DECORATE:
1 plum, cut into 4 slices
mint sprigs

Arrange the plums in a roasting tin and cook in a preheated oven, 200°C (400°F), Gas Mark 6, for 45 minutes.

Meanwhile, put the sugar, water, cinnamon stick and lemon peel into a saucepan. Slowly dissolve the sugar over a low heat and then bring to the boil. Cook over a medium heat for 20 minutes or until the mixture is syrupy.

Transfer the cooked plums to the sugar syrup and cook for a further 10 minutes. Remove the pan from the heat and discard the lemon peel and cinnamon stick.

Purée the fruit mixture in a blender or food processor. Alternatively, rub it through a sieve. Cool and freeze for 3 hours until just frozen. Remove from the freezer and mash with a fork. Return to the freezer for a further 3 hours.

Remove the sorbet from the freezer 10 minutes before you are ready to serve. Decorate with plum slices and mint sprigs.

COOK'S NOTES This sorbet is just as good made with lemons. Use 2 small lemons in place of the limes.

10 Cakes and Bakes

225 Irish soda bread

Preparation time:
15 minutes

Cooking time:
30 minutes

Oven temperature:
200°C (400°F)
Gas Mark 6

Makes:
1 medium loaf

250 g (8 oz) plain wholemeal flour
200 g (7 oz) plain white flour, plus extra
for dusting
½ teaspoon bicarbonate of soda
½ teaspoon cream of tartar
25 g (1 oz) butter
300 ml (½ pint) buttermilk or skimmed
milk

Sift together the two flours, bicarbonate of soda and cream of tartar, then rub in the butter until the mixture resembles fine breadcrumbs.

Quickly stir in the buttermilk or milk and mix until a soft dough is formed. Turn the dough on to a lightly floured work surface and knead until smooth.

Shape the dough into a round and place it on a lightly floured baking sheet. Cut a cross in the top with a sharp knife, sprinkle with a little flour, then bake in a preheated oven, 200°C (400°F), Gas Mark 6, for 25–30 minutes.

COOK'S NOTES This bread is very quick and simple to make as it does not contain any yeast, but relies on bicarbonate of soda to make it rise. It does not need proving – simply mix the ingredients and bake.

226 Plain crusty rolls

Preparation time:
25 minutes, plus
rising and proving

Baking time:
20 minutes

Oven temperature:
230°C (450°F)
Gas Mark 8

Makes:
about 18

15 g (½ oz) fresh yeast
450 ml (¾ pint) warm water
750 g (1½ lb) strong flour
15 g (½ oz) lard

Blend the yeast with one-third of the water. Sift the flour into a large bowl and rub in the lard. Make a well in the centre and pour in the yeast liquid and the remaining water. Mix to a soft dough then work with one hand until the dough leaves the sides of the bowl clean.

Turn out onto a lightly floured surface and knead for 10 minutes until smooth and elastic. Place in a clean warmed bowl, cover with a damp cloth and leave to rise in a warm place for 1 hour or until doubled in size.

Turn out and knead again for 2–3 minutes, then divide into 18 pieces. Roll each piece of dough into a ball between the floured palms of your hands. Press each one down on a pastry board, then release. Put the rolls on a lightly greased baking sheet, cover loosely with clingfilm and leave to rise. When ready the dough will spring back when pressed with a finger.

Remove the clingfilm and lightly brush the tops of the rolls with lightly salted water.

Bake in the centre of a preheated oven, 230°C (450°F), Gas Mark 8, for 20 minutes or until they sound hollow when tapped. Remove from the baking sheet and cool on a wire rack.

227 Basic brown bread   228 Garlic focaccia

227 Basic brown bread

Preparation time:
25 minutes, plus rising and proving

Baking time:
30–40 minutes

Oven temperature:
230°C (450°F)
Gas Mark 8

Makes:
1 large loaf or 10 rolls

750 g (1½ lb) strong wheatmeal flour
15 g (½ oz) salt
15 g (½ oz) lard or butter
15 g (½ oz) fresh yeast, or 2 teaspoons dried yeast mixed with 1 teaspoon caster sugar
575 ml (18 fl oz) warm water
caraway seeds (optional)

Mix the flour and salt in a large bowl. Add the fat and rub into the mixture. Blend the fresh yeast with the warm water. If you are using dried yeast follow the instructions on the packet or dissolve the sugar in the warm water, then sprinkle over the yeast. Set both types aside in a warm place for about 10 minutes or until it becomes frothy.

Use a wooden spoon to mix the yeast liquid into the flour. Continue to work the dough until it leaves the sides of the bowl clean. Turn out on to a clean board or work surface and knead thoroughly for about 10 minutes. Shape the dough into a ball and return to the bowl. Place the bowl inside a large polythene bag or cover it loosely with clingfilm and set it aside in a warm place until the dough has doubled in size.

Turn the risen dough on to a board or work surface and knock it back. Knead it again lightly. Grease and warm a 23 x 12 cm (9 x 5 inch) loaf tin or use ten mini tins. Shape the dough and allow it to rest again for about 10 minutes. Flatten the dough, then pull the sides over the centre and tuck over the ends. Put the dough in the tin or tins, smooth side up, and replace in the polythene bag or cover with clingfilm. Leave until the dough has risen to the tops of the tins. Bake in a preheated oven, 230°C (450°F), Gas Mark 8, for 30–40 minutes. For a soft crust, dust with flour before baking. For a crisp crust, brush with salted water.

228 Garlic focaccia

Preparation time:
20 minutes, plus standing

Cooking time:
25 minutes

Oven temperature:
220°C (425°F)
Gas Mark 7

Serves: **4–6**

5 g (¼ oz) dry yeast
1 teaspoon sugar
375 g (12 oz) plain flour
175 ml (6 fl oz) lukewarm water
1 teaspoon salt
3 garlic cloves, crushed
2 tablespoons olive oil, plus extra for greasing
1 tablespoon maize flour or semolina
2 teaspoons finely crushed sea salt

Combine the yeast, sugar, 1 teaspoon flour and water in a small mixing bowl. Stand, covered with clingfilm, in a warm place for 10 minutes or until foamy.

Sift the remaining flour and salt into a large bowl. Add the garlic and stir with a knife to combine. Make a well in the centre, stir in the yeast mixture and olive oil. Use a flat-bladed knife to mix to a firm dough.

Turn out the dough on to a lightly floured surface and knead for 10 minutes. Shape the dough into a ball and place it in a large, lightly oiled mixing bowl. Stand, covered with clingfilm, in a warm place for 40 minutes or until well risen.

Sprinkle the base of an 18 x 28 cm (7 x 11 inch) shallow baking tin with maize flour or semolina. Knead the dough again for 2 minutes or until smooth. Press the dough into the tin and prick holes with a skewer.

Sprinkle lightly with water and bake in a preheated oven, 220°C (425°F), Gas Mark 7, for 10 minutes and sprinkle again with water. Bake for a further 10 minutes, brush with extra olive oil, sprinkle with sea salt, then bake for 5 more minutes. Serve warm or at room temperature, cut into squares.

Preparation time:	**5 g (¼ oz) dry yeast**
20 minutes, plus	**1 teaspoon sugar**
standing	**375 g (12 oz) plain flour**
	175 ml (6 fl oz) lukewarm water
Cooking time:	**1 teaspoon salt**
25 minutes	**25 g (1 oz) Parmesan, finely grated**
	1 tablespoon finely chopped chives
Oven temperature:	**2 tablespoons olive oil, plus extra**
220°C (425°F)	**for brushing**
Gas Mark 7	**1 tablespoon maize flour or semolina**
	2 teaspoons finely crushed sea salt
Serves: **4–6**	

Combine the yeast, sugar, 1 teaspoon flour and water in small mixing bowl. Cover with clingfilm and leave to stand in a warm place for 10 minutes or until foamy.

Sift the remaining flour and salt into a large mixing bowl. Add the Parmesan and chives and stir with a flat-bladed knife to combine. Make a well in the centre and stir in the yeast mixture and olive oil. Use a knife to mix to a firm dough.

Turn out the dough on to a lightly floured surface and knead for 10 minutes. Shape the dough into a ball and place it in a large, lightly oiled mixing bowl. Cover with clingfilm and leave to stand in a warm place for 40 minutes or until well risen.

Sprinkle the base of an 18 x 28 cm (7 x 11 inch) shallow tin with maize flour or semolina. Knead the dough again for 2 minutes or until smooth. Press the dough into the tin and prick deep holes with a skewer. Sprinkle lightly with water and bake in a preheated oven, 220°C (425°F), Gas Mark 7, for 10 minutes. Sprinkle again with water and bake for a further 10 minutes. Brush with olive oil, sprinkle with sea salt and bake for 5 more minutes. Serve warm or at room temperature, cut into squares.

Preparation time:	**125 g (4 oz) strong white flour**
20 minutes, plus	**125 g (4 oz) plain flour**
rising and proving	**2 teaspoons salt**
	5 g (¼ oz) fresh yeast
Cooking time:	**1 teaspoon sugar**
10–13 minutes per	**300 ml (½ pint) warm milk and water**
batch	**1 tablespoon vegetable oil, plus extra**
	for greasing
Makes: **12–14**	**½ teaspoon bicarbonate of soda**
	150 ml (¼ pint) warm water

Sift the flours and salt into a warm bowl. Cream the yeast with the sugar, add the warmed milk and water and then the oil. Stir into the flour to make a batter and beat vigorously until smooth and elastic. Cover the bowl with clingfilm and leave it in a warm place until the mixture rises and the surface is full of bubbles, which will take about 1½ hours. Knock it back by beating with a wooden spoon.

Dissolve the bicarbonate of soda in the warm water and stir into the batter. Cover and leave in a warm place to prove for about 30 minutes.

To cook the crumpets, heat and grease a griddle or large frying pan. Grease five or six 8–9 cm (3–3½ inch) crumpet rings or scone cutters and put them on the griddle to heat.

Put 1 cm (½ inch) of batter into each ring. Cook gently for 7–10 minutes or until the surface sets and is full of tiny bubbles. Using an oven glove for protection, lift off the ring and, if the base of the crumpet is pale gold, flip it over and cook for another 3 minutes until the other side is just coloured.

If the crumpet batter is set but sticks slightly in the ring, push it out gently with the back of a wooden spoon. Wipe, grease and reheat the rings for each batch of crumpets.

COOK'S NOTES Cook as many crumpets as possible at a time bacause the batter will not remain bubbly for long, and should be used up as soon as possible.

231 Cheese scones

232 Oven scones

Preparation time: 12 minutes	250 g (8 oz) plain flour
	½ teaspoon salt
	1 teaspoon mustard powder
Cooking time: 10–15 minutes	4 teaspoons baking powder
	50 g (2 oz) butter or margarine
	75–125 g (3–4 oz) mature Cheddar, grated
Oven temperature: 220°C (425°F) Gas Mark 7	1 egg, beaten
	150 ml (¼ pint) milk or water
	TO FINISH:
Makes: about 12	milk
	grated cheese

Sift the flour, salt, mustard and baking powder into a mixing bowl. Cut the fat into the flour with a flat-bladed knife and then rub it in with your fingertips to a breadcrumb consistency. Mix in the grated cheese. Beat the egg with half the liquid and stir it into the dry ingredients. Work it into a soft dough, adding more liquid as necessary.

Turn the dough on to a well-floured board and roll out lightly until it is 1.5 cm (¼ inch) thick. Cut out rounds with a 6.5 cm (2½ inch) cutter. Work the remaining dough into a round and cut more rounds. Place all the rounds on a warmed baking sheet. Brush with milk and sprinkle with grated cheese.

Bake in a preheated oven, 220°C (425°F), Gas Mark 7, for 10–15 minutes until well risen and golden. Cool on a wire rack.

COOK'S NOTES Serve these scones with butter, cream cheese or a salad filling. They are also wonderful served warm from the oven, dripping in melting butter.

Preparation time: 12 minutes	250 g (8 oz) plain white or wheatmeal flour
	½ teaspoon salt
Cooking time: 7–10 minutes	4 teaspoons baking powder
	25–50 g (1–2 oz) butter or margarine
	150 ml (¼ pint) milk
Oven temperature: 230°C (450°F) Gas Mark 8	water, to mix
	milk or flour, to finish
	TO SERVE:
Makes: about 12	butter
	whipped cream
	strawberry jam

Sift the flour, salt and baking powder into a mixing bowl. Cut the fat into the flour with a flat-bladed knife then rub it in with your fingertips to a breadcrumb consistency. Make a well in the centre, pour in the milk and mix to a soft, spongy dough, adding a little water if necessary.

Turn the dough out on to a well-floured board and knead quickly and lightly. Roll out the dough with a floured rolling pin or flatten with floured hands until it is 1.5 cm (¾ inch) thick. Cut into rounds using a 6 cm (2½ inch) floured pastry cutter or a tumbler. Place the scones on a warmed baking sheet.

Shape the remaining dough into a ball, flatten into a circle, cut out more rounds and place on the baking sheet. Brush the scones with milk for a glazed finish or rub them with flour for a soft crust. Bake near the top of a preheated oven, 230°C (450°F), Gas Mark 8, for 7–10 minutes until well risen and golden on top.

To serve, split the scones and spread with butter, cream and jam.

233 Custard tarts

Preparation time:
30 minutes, plus cooling

Cooking time:
30–35 minutes

Oven temperature:
200°C (400°F) Gas Mark 6, then 160°C (325°F) Gas Mark 3

Makes: **8**

SWEET SHORTCRUST PASTRY:
250 g (8 oz) plain flour
pinch of salt
50 g (2 oz) butter
50 g (2 oz) lard or vegetable shortening
25 g (1 oz) caster sugar
1 egg yolk
water, to mix

CUSTARD:
450 ml (¾ pint) milk
2 eggs
2–3 teaspoons sugar
¼ teaspoon vanilla essence
grated nutmeg, to finish

Sift the flour and salt into a bowl. Rub the fat into the flour with your fingertips until the mixture resembles breadcrumbs, then mix in the sugar. Beat the egg yolk with 2 tablespoons of water and stir it into the flour mixture to make a fairly firm dough, adding a little more water as necessary. Knead lightly until smooth but do not overwork. Cover and leave to rest in the refrigerator for at least 30 minutes before rolling.

Grease 8 small, deep 5 cm (2 inch) muffin tins.

Roll out the cooked pastry thinly. Cut out 8 cm (3 inch) rounds and use them to line the muffin tins. Bake blind in a preheated oven, 200°C (400°F), Gas Mark 6, for 12–15 minutes until firm but not brown, then remove from the oven. Lower the heat to 160°C (325°F), Gas Mark 3.

To make the custard, warm the milk over a low heat and while it is heating beat together the eggs and sugar. Stir the warm milk into the beaten eggs and flavour with vanilla essence. Strain the custard into the partially baked cases.

Sprinkle the tops with grated nutmeg and return the tarts to the centre of the oven for 15–20 minutes until the custard is set. Serve cold.

234 Cream horns

Preparation time:
20 minutes, plus chilling

Cooking time:
15–20 minutes

Oven temperature:
220°C (425°F) Gas Mark 7

Makes: **10**

225 g (7½ oz) frozen puff pastry, defrosted
beaten egg, to glaze
5 tablespoons strawberry jam
175 ml (6 fl oz) double cream, whipped
glacé cherries, halved
angelica
icing sugar

Roll out the pastry into a rectangle about 25 x 33 cm (10 x 13 inches) and trim the edges. Cut into 10 strips, each 2.5 cm (1 inch) wide.

Dampen one long edge of each strip with water and wind round 10 cornet moulds, starting at the point and overlapping the dampened edge. Gently press the edges together. Place on a dampened baking sheet, cover and chill for 15 minutes.

Brush with egg and bake in a preheated oven, 220°C (425°F), Gas Mark 7, for 15–20 minutes until golden-brown. Leave for 5 minutes before carefully removing the moulds. Cool on a wire rack.

Spoon a little jam into each horn then pipe in the cream. Decorate with pieces of cherry and angelica and sprinkle with icing sugar.

COOK'S NOTES You will need 10 cornet moulds for these cream horns. They are simply metal cones, which the pastry is wrapped around and baked to make the horn shapes.

235 Victoria sandwich

Preparation time:
15 minutes

Cooking time:
20–25 minutes

Oven temperature:
180°C (350°F)
Gas Mark 4

Makes:
one 18 cm (7 inch)
cake

125 g (4 oz) butter or margarine
125 g (4 oz) caster sugar
2 eggs
125 g (4 oz) self-raising flour, sifted
1 tablespoon hot water

TO FINISH:
150 ml (¼ pint) double cream, lightly
  whipped
3 tablespoons jam
caster sugar, for sprinkling

Line and grease two 18 cm (7 inch) sandwich tins.

Cream the fat and sugar together until light and fluffy. Beat in the eggs, one at a time, adding a tablespoon of the flour with the second egg. Fold in the rest of the flour, then the water.

Divide the mixture between the prepared tins and bake in a preheated oven, 180°C (350°F), Gas Mark 4, for 20–25 minutes until the cakes are golden and spring back when lightly pressed with the fingers. Turn on to a wire rack to cool.

Sandwich the cakes together with the cream and jam and sprinkle the top with caster sugar.

COOK'S NOTES If you prefer, use butter icing to fill the cake. To make butter icing, beat 50 g (2 oz) of softened butter with 125 g (4 oz) of sifted icing sugar until smooth.

236 Genoese sponge

Preparation time:
15–20 minutes

Cooking time:
30–35 minutes

Oven temperature:
190°C (375°F)
Gas Mark 5

Makes:
one 23 cm (9 inch)
cake

50 g (2 oz) butter
4 eggs
125 g (4 oz) caster sugar
125 g (4 oz) plain flour, sifted

TO FINISH:
150 ml (¼ pint) double cream
2 tablespoons lemon curd
icing sugar, for sprinkling

Line and grease a 23 cm (9 inch) moule à manqué tin.

Warm the butter gently until just soft; take care that it does not become oily. Whisk the eggs and sugar in a mixing bowl over a saucepan of hot water until the mixture is thick enough to leave a trail. Remove from the heat and whisk until cool. You do not need to put the bowl over hot water if you are using an electric beater.

Fold in the flour. When it is almost incorporated, fold in the butter as rapidly as possible, being careful not to knock out the air. Turn immediately into the prepared tin and bake in a preheated oven, 190°C (375°F), Gas Mark 5, for 30–35 minutes or until the cake springs back when lightly pressed. Leave in the tin for 1 minute then turn on to a wire rack to cool.

Whip the cream until stiff then whisk in the lemon curd. Split the cake in half and sandwich together with the lemon cream. Sprinkle with icing sugar.

COOK'S NOTES A moule à manqué tin is a deep sandwich tin with slightly sloping sides. A standard cake tin could also be used.

237 Whisked sponge

238 Swiss roll

Preparation time:	**4 eggs**
15 minutes	**140 g (4½ oz) caster sugar**
	125 g (4 oz) plain flour, sifted
Baking time:	
35–40 minutes	TO FINISH:
	150 ml (¼ pint) double cream, whipped
Oven temperature:	**selection of fruit**
190°C (375°F)	**icing sugar, for sprinkling**
Gas Mark 5	
Makes:	
one 23 cm (9 inch)	
cake	

Preparation time:	**3 eggs**
15 minutes	**75 g (3 oz) caster sugar**
	75 g (3 oz) plain flour, sifted
Baking time:	**1 tablespoon hot water**
8–10 minutes	**3 tablespoons warmed jam**
	caster sugar, for dredging
Oven temperature:	
200°C (400°F)	
Gas Mark 6	
Makes:	
1 Swiss roll	

Line, grease and flour a 23 cm (9 inch) moule à manqué tin.

Whisk the eggs and sugar in a mixing bowl over a saucepan of boiling water until thick enough to leave a trail. Remove from the heat and whisk until cool. You do not need to put the bowl over hot water if you are using an electric beater.

Fold in the flour. Turn the mixture into the prepared tin and bake in a preheated oven, 190°C (375°F), Gas Mark 5, for 35–40 minutes or until the cake springs back when lightly pressed.

Turn on to a wire rack to cool. Split the cake in half and fill with the cream and three-quarters of the fruit. Arrange the remaining fruit on top and sprinkle with icing sugar.

Line and grease an 18 x 28 cm (7 x 11 inch) Swiss roll tin.

Whisk the eggs and sugar in a mixing bowl over a saucepan of hot water until thick enough to leave a trail. (Hot water is unnecessary if you are using an electric beater.) Fold in the flour and the water, then turn into the prepared Swiss roll tin.

Bake in a preheated oven, 200°C (400°F), Gas Mark 6, for 8–10 minutes until the cake springs back when lightly pressed.

Turn on to sugared greaseproof paper, peel off the lining paper and trim the edges. Cut a slit two-thirds of the way through the short edge nearest you, spread lightly with the jam and roll up quickly. Hold in position for a few minutes, then transfer the cake to a wire rack to cool. Dredge with caster sugar before serving.

COOK'S NOTES **The ideal whisk for this sponge is a wire balloon whisk because it incorporates so much air, although a hand-held electric beater is quicker.**

239 Angel cake

240 Madeira cake

Preparation time:	**25 g (1 oz) plain flour**
20 minutes	**25 g (1 oz) cornflour**
	150 g (5 oz) caster sugar
Baking time:	**5 large egg whites**
35–40 minutes	**1 teaspoon vanilla essence**
	150 ml (¼ pint) double cream, lightly
Oven temperature:	**whipped**
180°C (350°F)	**125 g (4 oz) raspberries**
Gas Mark 4	**50 g (2 oz) redcurrants**
	icing sugar, for sprinkling
Makes:	
one 20 cm (8 inch)	
cake	

Preparation time:	**175 g (6 oz) butter**
20 minutes	**175 g (6 oz) caster sugar**
	175 g (6 oz) self-raising flour
Baking time:	**75 g (3 oz) plain flour**
1¼ hours	**3 eggs**
	grated rind and juice of 1 lemon
Oven temperature:	
160°C (325°F)	
Gas Mark 3	
Makes:	
one 18 cm (7 inch)	
round cake or one	
1 kg (2 lb) loaf cake	

Sift the flours and 25 g (1 oz) of the caster sugar together three or four times. Whisk the egg whites until stiff, add the remaining caster sugar, a tablespoon at a time, and continue whisking until very thick.

Carefully fold in the sifted mixture with the vanilla essence and turn into a 20 cm (8 inch) angel cake tin. Smooth the surface and bake in a preheated oven, 180°C (350°F), Gas Mark 4, for 35–40 minutes until the cake springs back when lightly pressed.

Turn the cake upside down on a wire rack and leave in the tin until cold, when the cake will fall easily from the tin. Fill the well with the cream, raspberries and redcurrants and serve sprinkled with icing sugar.

Grease and line an 18 cm (7 inch) round cake tin or a 1 kg (2 lb) loaf tin.

Cream the butter with the sugar until light, fluffy and very pale.

Sift the self-raising and plain flours together. Beat the eggs into the creamed mixture, one at a time, following each addition with a spoonful of sifted flour.

Fold in the remaining flour, followed by the grated lemon rind and juice.

Bake in a preheated oven, 160°C (325°F), Gas Mark 3, for 1 hour or until well risen, firm to the touch and golden-brown.

Cool in the tin for 5–10 minutes, then turn on to a wire rack and leave until cold. Do not peel off the lining paper but wrap the cake as it is in foil or store in an airtight container until required.

COOK'S NOTES You will need a special angel cake tin in the shape of a ring to make this recipe. There is no need to grease it.

241 Cherry cake

Preparation time:	175 g (6 oz) butter or margarine
20 minutes	175 g (6 oz) caster sugar
	3 eggs
Baking time:	300 g (10 oz) self-raising flour, sifted
1½–2 hours	250 g (8 oz) glacé cherries, halved
	50 g (2 oz) ground almonds
Oven temperature:	about 5 tablespoons milk
160°C (325°F)	
Gas Mark 3	
Makes:	
one 18 cm (7 inch)	
cake	

Line and grease a deep 18 cm (7 inch) cake tin.

Cream the fat and sugar together until light and fluffy. Beat in the eggs one at a time, adding a tablespoon of flour with the last two.

Carefully fold in the remaining flour, then fold in the cherries, ground almonds and enough milk to give a dropping consistency.

Put the mixture into the prepared tin and bake in a preheated oven, 160°C (325°F), Gas Mark 3, for 1½–2 hours. Leave the cake in the tin for 5 minutes, then turn on to a wire rack to cool.

COOK'S NOTES Try to find the more natural, uncoloured glacé cherries for this cake as they will have a better flavour and colour.

242 Banana cake

Preparation time:	125 g (4 oz) butter or margarine
15 minutes	125 g (4 oz) caster sugar
	2 eggs
Baking time:	125 g (4 oz) self-raising flour, sifted
20–25 minutes	2 bananas, mashed
	icing sugar, to dust
Oven temperature:	
180°C (350°F)	FILLING:
Gas Mark 4	50 g (2 oz) ground almonds
	50 g (2 oz) icing sugar, sifted
Makes:	1 small banana, mashed
one 18 cm (7 inch)	1 teaspoon lemon juice
cake	

Line and grease two 18 cm (7 inch) sandwich tins.

Cream the fat and sugar together until light and fluffy. Add the eggs, one at a time, adding a tablespoon of flour with the second egg. Fold in the remaining flour with the bananas.

Divide the mixture between the prepared sandwich tins. Bake in a preheated oven, 180°C (350°F), Gas Mark 4, for 20–25 minutes until the cakes spring back when lightly pressed. Turn out the cakes on to a wire rack to cool.

To make the filling, mix the ground almonds with the icing sugar, add the banana and lemon juice and mix to a smooth paste. Sandwich the cakes together with the filling and dust with icing sugar.

243 Chocolate cake

244 Triple chocolate muffins

Preparation time:	**200 g (7 oz) plain flour**
15 minutes	**1 teaspoon bicarbonate of soda**
	1 teaspoon baking powder
Baking time	**2 tablespoons cocoa powder**
45–50 minutes	**150 g (5 oz) soft brown sugar**
	2 tablespoons golden syrup
Oven temperature:	**2 eggs**
160°C (325°F)	**150 ml (¼ pint) oil**
Gas Mark 3	**150 ml (¼ pint) milk**
Makes:	CHOCOLATE ICING:
one 23 cm (9 inch)	**175 g (6 oz) plain chocolate**
cake	**2 tablespoons single cream**
	TO DECORATE:
	75 g (3 oz) walnut halves
	icing sugar

Line and grease a 23 cm (9 inch) cake tin.

Sift the dry ingredients into a mixing bowl and make a well in the centre. Add the golden syrup, eggs, oil and milk and beat thoroughly until smooth.

Pour into the prepared tin and bake in a preheated oven, 160°C (325°F), Gas Mark 3, for 45–50 minutes. Leave the cake in the tin for a few minutes then turn on to a wire rack to cool.

To make the icing, put the chocolate and cream into a small saucepan and heat very gently until melted. Allow to cool slightly, then pour over the cake. Dredge the walnuts with icing sugar and arrange in the centre of the cake.

COOK'S NOTES Hazelnuts or pecan nuts could also be used to decorate the top of this cake.

Preparation time:	**300 g (10 oz) plain chocolate, chopped**
15 minutes	**50 g (2 oz) unsalted butter, melted**
	1 egg
Cooking time:	**350 ml (12 fl oz) milk**
25–30 minutes	**375 g (12 oz) self-raising flour**
	1 tablespoon baking powder
Oven temperature:	**50 g (2 oz) cocoa powder**
200°C (400°F)	**100 g (3½ oz) caster sugar**
Gas Mark 6	**50 g (2 oz) white chocolate buttons**
Makes: **12**	

Line a 12-cup deep bun tin with paper muffin cases.

Melt half the plain chocolate in a bowl over a saucepan of simmering water, then stir in the melted butter.

Beat together the egg and milk and stir this mixture into the melted chocolate. Sift the flour, baking powder and cocoa powder into a bowl. Stir in the sugar.

Add the liquid mixture to the dry ingredients, then stir in the remaining chocolate and the chocolate buttons.

Using a large metal spoon, gently fold the ingredients together until just combined. Divide the mixture among the paper cases. Bake in a preheated oven, 200°C (400°F), Gas Mark 6, for 20–25 minutes until well risen and just firm. Serve the muffins warm or cold.

Preparation time: **10 minutes**	**175 g (6 oz) unsalted butter, softened**
	250 g (8 oz) golden caster sugar
	125 g (4 oz) ground almonds
Cooking time: **30 minutes**	**2 eggs, beaten**
	finely grated rind and juice of 3 lemons
	75 g (3 oz) polenta flour
Oven temperature: **180°C (350°F)**	**50 g (2 oz) plain flour**
	½ teaspoon baking powder
Gas Mark 4	**2 tablespoons flaked almonds**
Serves: **6**	

Grease and line a 15 cm (6 inch) spring-form tin with greaseproof paper. Beat together the butter and 175 g (6 oz) of the sugar until pale and creamy. Stir in the almonds, eggs and rind and juice of 1 lemon.

Add the flours and baking powder, and stir in gently until combined. Turn into the tin, level the surface and sprinkle with the flaked almonds. Bake in a preheated oven, 180°C (350°F), Gas Mark 4, for about 30 minutes until risen and just firm.

Meanwhile, put the remaining lemon rind and juice in a small saucepan with the remaining sugar and heat gently until the sugar dissolves. Spoon over the cake and serve warm.

Preparation time: **15 minutes**	**175 g (6 oz) butter or margarine**
	175 g (6 oz) soft brown sugar
	3 large eggs
Cooking time: **1 hour**	**175 g (6 oz) wholemeal self-raising flour, or plain flour sifted with 1½ teaspoons baking powder**
Oven temperature: **180°C (350°F)**	**50 g (2 oz) ground almonds**
	175 g (6 oz) young carrots, finely grated
Gas Mark 4	**75 g (3 oz) walnuts, coarsely chopped**
Serves: **8**	**1 tablespoon milk**

Grease and flour or line a 20 cm (8 inch) deep cake tin.

Cream the butter or margarine and sugar until soft and light. Beat the eggs and gradually blend them into the creamed mixture.

Fold in the flour, or flour and baking powder, with the ground almonds.

Add the carrots, walnuts and milk. Mix thoroughly, then spoon into the prepared tin.

Bake in a preheated oven, 180°C (350°F), Gas Mark 4, for 1 hour or until firm to the touch. Leave to cool for 5 minutes in the tin.

Decorate when cool, if liked. Split the cake through the centre and spread with a good layer of cheese. Top with the rest of the cheese and scatter with chopped or halved walnuts.

COOK'S NOTES Quark, the slightly acidic German soft cheese, makes an excellent filling and topping for this carrot cake. Quark is generally available at large supermarkets.

247 Rich fruit cake

248 Chewy flapjack squares

Preparation time:	**250 g (8 oz) butter**
10–15 minutes	**250 g (8 oz) brown sugar**
	6 eggs
Cooking time:	**250 g (8 oz) plain flour**
3½ hours	**1½ teaspoons ground mixed spice**
	1 tablespoon cocoa powder
Oven temperature:	**grated rind and juice of 2 oranges**
160°C (325°F)	**grated rind and juice of 1 lemon**
Gas Mark 3,	**250 g (8 oz) currants**
then 150°C (300°F)	**250 g (8 oz) sultanas**
Gas Mark 2,	**250 g (8 oz) raisins**
then 140°C (275°F)	**175 g (6 oz) chopped mixed peel**
Gas Mark 1	**175 g (6 oz) glacé cherries, chopped**
	50 g (2 oz) blanched almonds, chopped
Makes:	
one 20 cm (8 inch)	TO COVER:
cake	**slightly warmed, sieved apricot jam**
	750 g (1½ lb) almond paste
	fondant icing

Line a deep 20 cm (8 inch) round cake tin with greaseproof paper and grease well.

Cream the butter and sugar together in a large bowl until they are fluffy and light in colour. Beat in the eggs, one at a time. Sift the flour with the spice and cocoa and stir in gradually. Stir in all the remaining ingredients and mix well.

Spoon the mixture into the prepared tin and spread evenly. Bake in a preheated oven, 160°C (325°F), Gas Mark 3, for 30 minutes. Reduce the oven temperature to 150°C (300°F), Gas Mark 2 and bake for a further 1 hour. Reduce the oven temperature to 140°C (275°F), Gas Mark 1 and bake for a further 2 hours or until cooked.

Turn the cake out to cool on a wire rack. Wrap the cake in greaseproof paper and foil and store for at least 1 month before using.

Brush the top and sides of the cake with the jam before covering with the rolled out almond paste and fondant icing.

Preparation time:	**75 g (3 oz) butter or margarine**
10 minutes	**175 g (6 oz) golden granulated sugar**
	125 g (4 oz) golden syrup
Cooking time:	**5 tablespoons milk**
40 minutes	**375 g (12 oz) rolled oats**
	500 g (1 lb) peeled cooking apples, cored
Oven temperature:	**and sliced**
180°C (350°F)	**25 g (1 oz) caster sugar**
Gas Mark 4	**¼ teaspoon ground cloves**
	2 tablespoons lemon juice
Makes:	
12 fingers	

Melt the butter or margarine in a saucepan with the sugar, syrup and milk. Stir in the oats. Spoon two-thirds of the mixture into a greased 18 cm (7 inch) shallow square tin and cook in a preheated oven, 180°C (350°F), Gas Mark 4, for 20 minutes.

Meanwhile, place the apples in a saucepan with the caster sugar, ground cloves and lemon juice and cook until thick and pulpy. Spread the apple over the cooked oat base. Spread the remaining oat mixture over the top and cook for a further 20 minutes. Allow to cool before cutting into 12 fingers.

COOK'S NOTES **You could try replacing the apples with a mixture of dried fruit and soft fruit such as peaches or plums.**

249 Mocha slices

Preparation time: **30 minutes**	**25 g (1 oz) butter** **2 eggs** **50 g (2 oz) caster sugar**
Cooking time: **25–30 minutes**	**50 g (2 oz) plain flour** **4 tablespoons apricot jam**
Oven temperature: **190°C (375°F)** **Gas Mark 5**	COFFEE BUTTER CREAM: **2 egg whites** **125 g (4 oz) icing sugar, sifted** **125 g (4 oz) unsalted butter**
Makes: **10**	**1 tablespoon coffee essence**

COFFEE ICING:
250 g (8 oz) icing sugar, sifted
2 teaspoons coffee essence
1½ tablespoons water

Line and grease an 18 cm (7 inch) square shallow tin. Prepare the sponge as for Genoese Sponge (see recipe 236). Turn the mixture into the prepared tin and bake in a preheated oven, 190°C (375°F), Gas Mark 5, for 25–30 minutes. Turn on to a wire rack to cool, then cut it in half.

To make the coffee butter cream, whisk the egg whites and sugar together over a saucepan of simmering water until the mixture holds its shape. Cool slightly. Cream the butter until soft, then add the meringue mixture a little at a time. Stir in the coffee essence.

Use some of the butter cream to sandwich the cake halves together, then cut the cake into 10 fingers.

Warm the jam in a small saucepan, then press it through a sieve into a bowl. Brush the apricot glaze over the fingers to coat them completely. Leave to set.

To make the icing, combine the icing sugar, coffee essence and water. Spread the icing evenly over the fingers and leave to set.

Pipe the remaining butter cream in a zigzag along the middle of each slice.

250 Fresh lemon slices

Preparation time: **15 minutes**	**250 g (8 oz) butter or margarine, softened** **75 g (3 oz) icing sugar** **1 teaspoon vanilla essence**
Cooking time: **about 40 minutes**	**250 g (8 oz) plain flour** **4 eggs** **175 g (6 oz) granulated sugar**
Oven temperature: **190°C (375°F)** **Gas Mark 5**	**grated rind of 1 lemon** **6 tablespoons lemon juice**
Makes: **36**	

Generously grease a 30 x 23 cm (12 x 9 inch) shallow baking tin.

Put the butter, 50 g (2 oz) of the icing sugar and the vanilla essence into a bowl and cream until light and fluffy. Sift the flour and fold, a little at a time, into the creamed mixture until completely incorporated. Turn the mixture into the prepared tin and spread it to make the surface even. Bake in a preheated oven, 190°C (375°F), Gas Mark 5, for 20 minutes.

Meanwhile put the eggs, granulated sugar, lemon rind and lemon juice into a bowl. Stir to blend the ingredients but do not beat. Pour the mixture over the baked pastry layer.

Return the tin to the oven and bake for 18–22 minutes until the topping is set and lightly browned.

Remove the tin from the oven and sift the remaining icing sugar over the warm cake to cover it generously. Cut the cake into slices. Remove from the tin when cool.

COOK'S NOTES You could replace the lemon rind and juice in this recipe with the rind of 2 limes and 6 tablespoons lime juice.

251 Butter shortbread

252 French honey and fruit biscuits

Preparation time:
15–20 minutes

Cooking time:
30–35 minutes

Oven temperature:
160°C (325°F)
Gas Mark 3

Serves: **8–10**

125 g (4 oz) plain flour
50 g (2 oz) cornflour
50 g (2 oz) caster sugar
125 g (4 oz) butter, plus extra for greasing

Sift together the flour and cornflour. Add the sugar and rub in the butter. The mixture will become crumbly at first, but continue rubbing with your fingertips until it clings together in heavy clumps.

Turn on to a board or work surface lightly dusted with flour or cornflour and knead lightly. Roll out to a 20 cm (8 inch) circle and place on a greased baking sheet. Prick all over the top with a fork, mark into 8 or 10 portions and flute the edges with your fingers.

Bake in a preheated oven, 160°C (325°F), Gas Mark 3, for 30–35 minutes until the shortbread is cooked but not brown. Leave on the baking sheet for 10 minutes, then lift off with a fish slice and place carefully on a wire rack to cool completely. Break into portions to serve.

Preparation time:
15 minutes, plus soaking

Cooking time:
10–12 minutes

Oven temperature:
190°C (375°F)
Gas Mark 5

Makes:
about 9

75 g (3 oz) glacé or crystallized fruit, finely chopped
1 tablespoon rum
125 g (4 oz) plain flour
50 g (2 oz) butter
1 small egg
50 g (2 oz) caster sugar
a few drops of vanilla essence
3–4 tablespoons thick honey
icing sugar, for dusting

Soak the fruit in the rum for at least 30 minutes.

Sift the flour into a bowl and add the butter. Mix together quickly by hand and make a well in the centre. Add the egg, sugar and vanilla essence and blend the ingredients together. Roll into a smooth ball, wrap in clingfilm and chill for 30 minutes.

Roll out the pastry, sprinkle with the fruit, fold it up and knead lightly until the fruit is well mixed into the dough. Roll out fairly thinly and cut into 5 cm (2 inch) rounds.

Place the rounds on a greased baking sheet and bake in a preheated oven, 190°C (375°F), Gas Mark 5, for 10–12 minutes until set and golden. Cool on a wire rack and sandwich together in pairs with honey. To serve, dust lightly with sieved icing sugar.

COOK'S NOTES **If you want to make shortbread fingers, press the mixture into a greased square tin and mark into fingers before cooking.**

253 Bittersweet biscuits

254 Almond butter cookies

Preparation time:
20 minutes

Cooking time:
10–12 minutes

Oven temperature:
190°C (375°F)
Gas Mark 5

Makes:
about 36

200 g (7 oz) plain flour
¼ teaspoon salt
¼ teaspoon bicarbonate of soda
¼ teaspoon baking powder
1 tablespoon instant coffee granules
125 g (4 oz) butter or margarine, softened
50 g (2 oz) vegetable cooking fat
125 g (4 oz) granulated sugar
125 g (4 oz) soft brown sugar
1½ teaspoons vanilla essence
1 egg yolk
about 3 tablespoons granulated sugar
50 g (2 oz) chocolate coffee beans

Preparation time:
20 minutes, plus
cooling

Cooking time:
14–16 minutes

Oven temperature:
160°C (325°F)
Gas Mark 3

Makes:
about 36

175 g (6 oz) plain flour
½ teaspoon baking powder
125 g (4 oz) butter or margarine, softened
75 g (3 oz) sugar
½ teaspoon vanilla essence
2 tablespoons water

PRALINE:
125 g (4 oz) sugar
25 g (1 oz) almonds

Sift the flour, salt, bicarbonate of soda, baking powder and instant coffee into a bowl and set aside.

Put the butter or margarine and cooking fat into a large bowl and cream until light and fluffy. Add the sugars and beat until well blended. Beat in the vanilla essence and then the egg yolk. Gradually add the flour mixture, beating until just well combined.

Shape the mixture into 2.5 cm (1 inch) balls and place them about 5 cm (2 inches) apart on ungreased baking sheets. Dip a tumbler in granulated sugar and use it to flatten each biscuit to 5 mm (¼ inch) thick. Press a chocolate coffee bean in the centre of each one.

Bake the biscuits in a preheated oven, 190°C (375°F), Gas Mark 5, for 10–12 minutes until they are golden-brown and firm to the touch. Leave to cool on the baking sheets for 1–2 minutes, then transfer them to wire racks to cool completely.

To make the praline, put the sugar and almonds in a small, heavy-based saucepan over medium-high heat and stir occasionally until the sugar dissolves and turns a pale amber colour.

Pour out the caramel mixture on to a greased and lined baking sheet to make a layer 5 mm (¼ inch) thick; spread it out with an oiled palette knife. Set aside until cold.

Break the praline into pieces and put them into a polythene bag. Crush the pieces coarsely with a rolling pin.

Sift the flour and baking powder into a bowl, then set aside. Put the butter and sugar in a large bowl and cream until light and fluffy. Add the vanilla essence and mix well.

Add the flour mixture alternately with the water, mixing until smooth after each addition. Stir the crushed praline into the mixture.

Drop rounded teaspoonfuls, 5 cm (2 inches) apart, on to well-greased baking sheets. Bake in a preheated oven, 160°C (325°F), Gas Mark 3, for 14–16 minutes or until the edges are lightly browned. Leave the cookies on the baking sheets for 2 minutes, then carefully transfer to wire racks to cool completely.

COOK'S NOTES If you can't get chocolate-covered coffee beans, plain coffee beans could be used instead.

255 Vanilla and sesame wafers

256 Japonais

Preparation time:
20 minutes

Cooking time:
15–18 minutes

Oven temperature:
160°C (325°F)
Gas Mark 3

Makes:
about 48

50 g (2 oz) sesame seeds
65 g (2½ oz) plain flour
¼ teaspoon baking powder
¼ teaspoon salt
125 g (4 oz) butter or margarine, softened
125 g (4 oz) soft brown sugar
1 egg
1 teaspoon vanilla essence

Preparation time:
15 minutes

Cooking time:
30–35 minutes

Oven temperature:
150°C (300°F)
Gas Mark 2

Makes: **8**

50 g (2 oz) ground almonds
125 g (4 oz) caster sugar
2 egg whites

COFFEE BUTTER ICING:
40 g (1½ oz) butter
75 g (3 oz) icing sugar, sifted
1 teaspoon milk
1 teaspoon coffee essence

TO FINISH:
25 g (1 oz) ground almonds, toasted
icing sugar, to dust

Spread the sesame seeds in a shallow tin and bake in a preheated oven, 160°C (325°F), Gas Mark 3, stirring occasionally, for 6–8 minutes or until lightly toasted. Set aside.

Sift the flour, baking powder and salt into a bowl, then set aside.

Cream the butter and brown sugar in a bowl until light and fluffy. Beat in the egg, add the vanilla essence and mix well.

Gradually add the flour mixture until just blended. Add the roasted sesame seeds and stir until well combined.

Place rounded teaspoonfuls, about 5 cm (2 inches) apart, on greased baking sheets. Bake in the oven for 9–10 minutes or until the biscuits are lightly browned.

Mix together the almonds and sugar and set aside. Whisk the egg whites until stiff, then fold in the almond mixture. Spoon the mixture into a piping bag fitted with a 1 cm (½ inch) plain nozzle and pipe sixteen 5 cm (2 inch) rounds on a piece of nonstick paper placed on a baking sheet.

Bake in a preheated oven, 150°C (300°F), Gas Mark 2, for 30–35 minutes. Transfer to a wire rack.

To make the coffee butter icing, cream the fat with half the icing sugar until soft, then add the milk, coffee essence and the remaining icing sugar. Beat well.

Sandwich the rounds together in pairs with some of the butter icing and spread more round the sides.

Press ground almonds round the side of each cake. Leave to set, then dust with icing sugar.

COOK'S NOTES The biscuits will be very fragile when they first come out of the oven, so leave them on the baking sheets to cool for a few minutes, then carefully transfer them to wire racks.

Index

Acknowledgements

Photographs are in source order by recipe number.

OCTOPUS PUBLISHING GROUP LIMITED/Nick Carman97 **/Jean Cazals** 32, 51, 86, 108, 132, 146, 157, 161, 162, 164 /**Stephen Conroy** 110, 198, 199, 201, 209, 218 /**Jeremy Hopley** 211 /**David Jordan** 35, 147, 153, 204 /**Graham Kirk** 58, 186, 190, 217 /**Sandra Lane** 4, 23, 28, 36, 78, 111, 112, 127 /**William Lingwood** 68, 73, 75, 76, 77, 85, 113, 152, 154, 216, 222, 228, 229, 246 /**David Loftus** 104, 121, 168, 187 /**James Merrell** 194 /**Neil Mersh** 207 /**Diana Miller** 2, 15 /**Hilary Moore** 20, 45, 53, 82, 84, 90, 93, 94, 115 /**David Munns** 8 /**James Murphy** 88 /**Peter Myers** 26, 62, 69, 70, 71, 87, 89, 91, 131, 178 /**Sean Myers** 3, 13, 34, 37, 38, 40, 46, 49, 59, 61, 63, 64, 123, 126, 134, 193, 215, 219 /**William Reavell** 14, 16, 22, 25, 101, 102, 103, 105, 130, 149, 150, 200, 203, 213, 225 /**Craig Robertson** 208, 245 /**Simon Smith** 1, 5, 6, 7, 9, 10, 11, 17, 21, 24, 27, 33, 52, 54, 56, 57, 65, 66, 67, 74, 79, 81, 92, 95, 96, 98, 99, 100, 107, 116, 120, 125, 128, 135, 138, 139, 141, 142, 148, 151, 156, 158, 160, 165, 167, 170, 172, 174, 175, 176, 177, 179, 180, 181, 182, 183, 184, 185, 188, 189, 192, 195, 196, 197, 205, 212, 214, 221, 223, 224, 226, 227, 230, 231, 232, 233, 234, 235, 236, 237, 238, 239, 240, 241, 242, 243, 244, 247, 248, 249, 250, 251, 252, 253, 254, 255, 256 /**Roger Stowell** 206 /**Ian Wallace** 19, 60, 80, 114, 155, 169, 202, 210 /**Philip Webb** 12, 18, 30, 31, 39, 41, 42, 43, 44, 47, 48, 50, 55, 72, 109, 117, 118, 119, 122, 124, 129, 133, 136, 137, 140, 143, 144, 145, 159, 163, 166, 171, 173, 194, 220